Althar

Opus Magnum

Joachim Wolffram

Editor: Tess Henry

The Althar series consists of:
Volume 1: "Althar – The Crystal Dragon"
Volume 2: "Althar – The New Magi"
Volume 3: "Althar – Towards Utopia"
Volume 4: "Althar – The Final Letting Go"
Volume 5: "Althar – Opus Magnum"

Also available from Joachim Wolffram:
"Althar Intense – Space, Time, Veiling"
"For You – Records from Your Lives"
"The Free Human"

**For information about audio recordings
and workshops please visit:**
www.wolffram.de
or
facebook.com/joachim.wolffram

Contents

1. Liberating Illusions

I am Althar, the Crystal Dragon!

Welcome back, dear friend! It is once again a great honor and joy to be with you. I would like to begin by expressing my deep gratitude for allowing me to be part of your journey. Nothing emits more beauty than a consciousness that is blossoming towards its unlimited, natural state. Even though it can rightfully be said that your journey through separation is already over, a part of you is still rubbing your eyes in amazement, not yet fully realizing the overwhelming magnitude of your endeavor. But those observing you from outside the physical, whether they have ascended or not, *do* know, and they are already applauding you.

After this very honest, albeit somewhat schmaltzy preliminary remark, let us dive directly and joyfully into this fifth series of messages with a shocking announcement:

This will be the final volume!

From the outset, the Althar series was meant to become a concise handbook of enlightenment and embodied ascension, bundling all relevant information in a single and easily accessible place. Enlightenment and to some extent, embodied ascension have been discussed throughout the ages in a wide variety of traditions using different terminologies. We have tried to explain both topics in a modern language, free of all distracting reverence and annoying references to all the great and mostly dead masters of the past.

Concise implies that the Althar book series does not become an endless story that feeds the reader striving for enlightenment with a steady stream of spiritual popcorn. Thus, this volume will be the final volume. Final in the sense that with the following discussions we will have covered the entire spectrum of what I, and those who support me, consider relevant to realize enlightenment and embodied ascension.

In the future, we may choose to discuss some topics again from a different perspective in order to make them clearer or more practicable. We could also discuss additional details or practical problems that arise in the process of embodied ascension. But as far as the *universal* insights, knowledge and wisdom that we consider necessary are concerned – *this is it!* In other words, there is nothing hidden from you. Now it is only up to you – more than ever.

The good news is that we have quite a bit on the plate, and in a way, no mouth is large enough to take it all in at once. Hence, I predict that you will reread this book several times. Ideally, you will gain a deeper and deeper understanding until you can finally confirm *within yourself* what we are trying to convey.

In the previous volume, we spoke about the final letting go. We named the letting go of the belief in separation the *one and only letting go of real importance.* However, as exciting as letting go of separation may sound, it implies some tremendous consequences. These are often more than overwhelming for a consciousness that is still bound to the ways of humans – especially when this consciousness is about to *embody* these very consequences.

Therefore, we will take a closer look at some of these consequences. Thus, we arrive in a natural way and with all due modesty at what in the past was called "Opus Magnum – The Great Work." This term was used by the true alchemists who dared to transform the human self into divine beingness.

The realization of divine beingness equals the realization of embodied ascension – that is the Opus Magnum, *and we strive for nothing less!* Thus, the Opus Magnum can be regarded as the capstone of our messages.

To get to this central turning point in consciousness, we will take a deep look at the main reason why maintaining the natural, unlimited state of consciousness during incarnation is so difficult and almost impossible. To this end, we will examine in detail what underlies the process of incarnation and dive deeply into the subatomic structure of the physical.

Finally, we will connect a number of dots laid out throughout the Althar book series and unite them into an overview.

Before we start, let me make it once again totally clear that nothing I state is meant as dogma or as some kind of ultimate truth. Instead, my remarks are just another attempt to *dissolve illusions with the help of liberating illusions!* What else could one do? If someone is caught in an illusionary web of beliefs, patterns, and distorted notions, it is not of much help to just advise, "Let go!" Instead, one must find helpful symbols and means so that the person *accepts and applies* the remedy of letting go.

Hence, we have and must continue to speak of certain topics *as if they were real* – as we have done with energy, for example. Energy is *the* hot topic of humans. They want to *have* it, they want to *direct* it, they want to be *immune* to it. And if you experience the Second Round of Creation from within a body, not being aware of the scene spheres you are constantly traversing, energy seems to be so omnipresent that of course you take it as real. So, we had to use the term energy until we finally arrived at a point where we could just get rid of it.

The very same holds for *any* notion resulting from separation. Thus, even in this final volume, we will use some terms *as if they were real*, until we finally reach the end of separation, where all notions simply lose their relevance. For instance, we will talk about the "micro level of consciousness" and emphasize its very important role within separation. Within pure consciousness, however, there is quite obviously *no level whatsoever,* so a "micro level of consciousness" cannot be found there.

As soon as the final letting go is realized by a human, the liberating illusions that have brought him there become kind of irrelevant. So there is no reason to cling to the symbols I use! They are meant for liberation, not for solidifying separation. However, it may well be that the same liberating illusions are also helpful for other people – then of course it makes sense to use them further and to refine them if necessary.

Throughout the following messages, two remarkable entities will accompany us, although the term "entity" does not exactly apply to them. Both will play an important role in what I am trying to convey, and they will be very accessible to you, dear reader, not only while you are reading, but also afterwards. Both will be introduced in more detail in later chapters, but I want to prepare the ground for them from the beginning by mentioning them here.

As usual, at the end of an introduction, I provide my consistently ignored advice *not to rush through the text,* but to *read only one chapter per day!* I know, you most likely won't even notice this paragraph, but don't blame me if this accounts for a few more lives on your part. And then we will have to go over it all over again – just like this time. Remember?

I am Althar, Draco Crystallinus sum.

2. The Eye of Suchness

I am Althar, the Crystal Dragon!

Consciousness is indeed fascinating. Even if it expresses itself only through separation, it brings forth marvelous phenomena. Seen from the highest level, separation is just an instantaneous pondering of an impossible state. But as soon as you experience this pondering from within and act out the impossibility, it appears to be incredibly real.

In its utmost extreme, the exploration of separation leads you into a physical body, bound by skin. This represents life at the lower end of the spectrum of consciousness. What is "inside" and what is "outside" the body is clearly defined. To ensure its survival, the body registers every touch of its skin, and if necessary, transforms it into severe pain. Thus, the physical body can be seen as *the* symbol of separation par excellence.

Sure, at times a human may feel expanded beyond his corporeal limits, but as soon as his physical body is threatened, he usually returns to survival mode immediately and will do anything to protect his flesh and bones.

Together with the physical body, its sense organs appear, which are actually *instruments of separation*. Each sense organ reacts to certain objects on the outside as soon as it is stimulated by radiation or a reflection of those objects, be it light, sound waves, molecules, or touch. Then, the sensory organ reacts and transforms the received impulses into an inner representation of the apparent outside world. This transformation is automatically accompanied by an evaluation based on past experiences, desires, and fears. Thus, it is obvious that perception based on these sense organs is very limited, personal, and therefore, *utterly distorted!*

That is why I say:

You cannot perceive reality as it really is through your sense organs!

Therefore, I denote the physical eye, which represents the dominant sense of humans, the *Eye of Separation.*

The human uses almost exclusively the Eye of Separation for perception, and thereby *permanently solidifies the illusion of being a separate entity.*

But there is another way of perceiving reality! There is an eye that has neither form nor limitation. An eye that *simply knows.* It knows things *as they truly are.* It *knows* that every appearance is a formation of an immeasurable, *unlimited* consciousness that explores limitation.

This eye is not personal. It has no history. It has neither fears nor desires. It does not deform phenomena by projections or associations. Thus, *it sees things as they truly are!* It sees them *undistorted.* This eye I call:

The Eye of Suchness.

*

The Eye of Suchness is one with your natural state as a sovereign creator being. Thus, to apply it corresponds to your true nature and is therefore *nothing you need to learn!* However, since you have been in separation for so long, the Eye of Suchness has been veiled, barricaded, and forgotten. It was overlaid by the Eye of Separation.

How can you permanently expose your Eye of Suchness?

By cultivating your awareness. By choosing to be the *observer* of what *seems* to be happening. By no longer cooperating with the autopilot that drives your life through impulses, patterns, fears, desires, and false identities. By consciously doing all of this again and again *as soon as you realize that you have once more been sucked back into the dream of separation and see it as real!*

Whether you like it or not, as a limited human being, you actually have but a *single choice of real importance* to make! The choice is this:

Do you want to perceive with the Eye of Separation or with the Eye of Suchness?

Or to put it another way:

Do you want to solidify separation or go beyond it?

This choice is yours; only *you* can make it – and you have to make it *every single moment!*

*

My messages are all based on three pillars that are closely connected to the Eye of Suchness. Thus, choosing the Eye of Suchness represents *the essence of all my messages.*

The first pillar is *true wisdom.* True wisdom contains the power to lead one beyond separation. This wisdom makes it possible to see clearly, for it dissolves all distortions.

The second pillar is *true practice.* A practice of non-doing, not identifying, and letting go of whatever you perceive. A practice that does not ask for results, but *is* already the result in itself. A practice that simply allows the full awareness of pure consciousness.

The third pillar *is true compassion.* A compassion that is unconditional for it knows *separation is not real,* and thus, nothing has ever *really* happened. True compassion comes from *beyond* separation. It asks for nothing. It does not make any event "real" by focusing on it. It is utterly *unconditional.*

By choosing the Eye of Suchness, you *instantly* bring all three pillars to life!

Choosing the Eye of Suchness is *true practice.* It resembles a moment of spontaneous enlightenment. Why? Because a moment in which you choose the Eye of Suchness is a *moment of realization of your true nature!* It is *not a doing,* it is a choice *to be aware of* true reality.

The clarity of the Eye of Suchness may only last for a short while before it is again obscured by thoughts, emotions, and false identities. But in this moment of clarity, *you can become aware of the interpretations you add to your perceptions and instantly let them go!*

For a moment, you can once again see or at least guess that in true reality, there is no separation between you and what you have perceived. By repeatedly letting go of the distortions you have added, you soften the walls of separation. That is applied *true wisdom.*

Choosing the Eye of Suchness is *true compassion,* for it *instantly stops you from judging or rejecting* yourself or others. What is that supposed to help anyway? Whatever seems to have happened in the dream of separation *has never really happened.* So there is no reason to *grant reality* to an event through distorted compassion. Based on true compassion, you can decide unbiasedly what to do in a given situation.

Thus, by choosing the Eye of Suchness, you *embody* all three pillars, and beyond that, *you are instantly in suchness yourself!* Just like that! And *to be in suchness is the natural state of an enlightened being.*

Walking in suchness in the appearance of a human body is the bringing of light into an unreal world that is falsely perceived as real. It is the light of wisdom that dissolves all boundaries and imaginary differences. A human in suchness is like a loving reminder that inspires the beings living in separation to gently wake up from a dream that *had* to be dreamed – simply because it could be dreamed.

I am Althar, a cosmic optician.

3. The Creation of Scene Spheres

I am Althar, the Crystal Dragon!

In the last volume I made a note about scene spheres, which probably caused some frowning. I said when pure consciousness reflected on separation, it dreamed all imaginable scene spheres into place. In a manner of speaking, they were born *instantaneously, completely, and simultaneously.*

Furthermore, I said that for exactly this reason there is *no true creation* within separation. For no matter how immensely great the worlds of separation may seem, *within separation there is nothing but separation,* and thus exclusively the repetition of the same polarity-based plots.

Since it is so important and helpful to grasp these insights in all their implications, I will now try to shed a little more light on the underlying principles. To do so, I will use an analogy that I hope will help make my statements comprehensible. Since I'm trying to illustrate one analogy, that of the scene spheres, by means of another analogy, we're obviously moving on some bumpy terrain. But so be it! This is not about satisfying sophistic philosophers, but about preparing the ground for *experiencing* true wisdom.

Before we get started, I'd like to remind you what a scene sphere is. A scene sphere represents the totality of all perceptions, including the thoughts, emotions, and feelings that a being has at a given moment. I imagine it as a ball into which a consciousness can immerse and then experience it *from within.* As consciousness then progresses from sphere to sphere, it creates the feeling of being subject to a linear passage of time.

As an analogy, let us now have a look at the well-known game of chess. Take a square board, divide it into 64 equally sized squares, add a few pieces, define the goal of the game, and determine the moves allowed for each piece – and there we have "the royal game." But by simply defining the rules much more has happened! In fact, *all playable chess games automatically burst into existence!* They are *just there!* They arise with the definition of the rules, and one could enumerate them with a simple algorithm one after the other.

"But where are they?" one might ask. "Are they stored somewhere on a cosmic hard drive? Are they constantly kept alive by an ominous chess spirit?" Not at all! They exist *implicitly*, as a mathematician would say. One cannot see the chess games or locate them in any way, but nevertheless the totality of all possible games exists implicitly and fully automatically, only by the definition of the chess rules.

Now let's take a look at a few numbers to get a feeling for the immensity of what we are talking about here. As mentioned, one could easily enumerate all possible chess games, but in this example we will limit ourselves to games with no more than forty moves. Clever minds have determined that this results in about 10^{115} possible games. That's a 1, followed by 115 zeros.

Imagine we wanted to represent these potential games explicitly for whatever reason. Fortunately, we have a high-tech device at hand that allows us to inscribe a complete game in a single atom. So, we would only need an appropriate number of atoms and a small program to enumerate the games, and we would be done.

Unfortunately, physicists let us know that the universe known to humans consists of only 10^{78} atoms. So not only are there too few atoms in the universe to store all the games, *there are way, way, way too few!* Well, for creators this is not exactly a problem – we could simply create another 10^{37} universes of the same size and get started, couldn't we?

The points I want to make are these: With the definition of the chess rules, *all* potential games are created – and their number is *gigantic!* The term "ocean of oceans" does not even come close to describing these orders of magnitude. Moreover, for these potential games to exist, neither an explicit representation nor the unimaginable time to enumerate them all are necessary. Instead, they exist implicitly. They arise with the rules of the game. Just like that!

*

Now imagine that every possible position of the chess pieces corresponds exactly to one scene sphere. Then, dive into such a sphere and experience it *from within*. Become a queen, a king, or a pawn. How does this world feel? You have companions around you who are white or black just like you. There is a certain selection of moves that could be made with you. On the playing field you are able to feel all kinds of emotions like tension, hope, or fear. In addition, there is a hidden power that literally captures you every now and then and actually sets you on a new field.

Now, let's expand consciousness a little. Instead of "incarnating" into a single figure, dive into a scene sphere and simultaneously become all the white or black figures. Imagine that you are the power that moves the figures, plans, maneuvers, sets traps, and experiences the tension of the game. Starting from the current sphere, you can move to one of the permitted next spheres according to the rules. As you do this, you immerse yourself more and more in the world of chess.

You recognize nuances and schemes that you have missed before. The complexity of the game increasingly takes you over and demands everything from you. You want to win, or at least stay in the game for a long time. You want to try new strategies. You want revenge for lost games. You want to experience the feeling of winning again and again. More and more, you forget that there is also an existence outside the chess spheres.

By immersing yourself in a chess sphere, *you bring it to life*. With each game you play, you participate in new experiences and perhaps even become a master of chess. Thereby, you continuously create your thread of time by navigating through the ocean of chess scene spheres move by move. However:

You don't create a single new chess sphere!

They all existed already. You may experience a position for the first time, but you certainly did not *create* it! Within separation, there is simply *no true creation* – and therefore not in chess either!

As soon as this slowly dawns on you, you could try to experience something "new" by playing especially abstruse moves. But no matter how often, or in whichever way you play in the world of chess, *you will always only encounter chess positions!*

In other words:

You cannot go beyond the world of chess by continuing to play chess!

How long can you play chess until you recognize the constant repetition despite the countless variations? How long can you then blandish the game until you realize that you are only cheating yourself?

And would anything change if you modified the rules? Maybe with a few additional fields or a new figure?

Nothing would change at all! Again, all possible games would be created automatically and the same drives such as wanting to win or wanting revenge would be acted out.

That is the essence of all games in separation – *there is simply nothing new.*

*

The idea of separation could also be seen as a game. A game with exactly *one rule.* This rule states that any intent of pure consciousness can only be experienced by means of separation, which can be applied arbitrarily often unto itself. That is all! Finito! And just like in chess, *all possible scene spheres of separation suddenly exist!*

Of course, they are *immeasurably more extensive* than the handful of potential games of chess. If one absolutely wanted to imagine them – which I strongly advise against, because the human mind would simply be overwhelmed with it – then the chess spheres would only be a miniscule accumulation somewhere within the scene spheres of separation.

But no matter how large the number of scene spheres of separation may be, just as in chess you will never *create anything new* from within separation, because everything based on separation *is already there!* You merely navigate through some of these spheres, creating your thread of time that seems to span eons.

In addition, as in chess, there is no way to go beyond separation *by continuing to play the game of separation!*

Within separation, your patterns, desires, and fears are the impulses that push you ever further into the next scene sphere. One could say that they determine your possible moves. When you then at some point announce to yourself, "Enough is enough!" and long for enlightenment, but believe you can realize it by "doing" something, it only becomes just another impulse that drives you through the scene spheres of separation.

Therefore, I repeat: *No "doing" will ever set you free from separation!*

It is *true wisdom* that makes you realize that you are actually not *trapped* in separation! Because it is *you* who constantly projects yourself into the scene spheres of separation, forgetting your true nature. It is true wisdom, paired with the constant non-doing of letting go, that will slowly but surely set you free.

By choosing the Eye of Suchness again and again, you increasingly see things as they truly are and *free yourself from the belief in separation.* While you free yourself more and more from compulsive drives, you create ever-more leeway for your performance on the stage of separation.

Then one day, you will have to choose whether you want to exist simultaneously within and without separation. By then, you will have completely let go of the belief in separation and will no longer be subject to any rules. You could become a New Magi, moving freely through the worlds of separation at will.

*

This seems to me to be the right opportunity to reformulate an earlier statement with our current expanded understanding. At that time I said, "dragons guide energies." Back then, this was a very appropriate statement. But in the meantime, we have come so far that we have even gone beyond the notion of energy as understood by humans. *There is no energy!* Only when crossing scene spheres does energy *seem* to be very real, just as time seems to be very real. From the perspective of true reality, however, energy is just another symptom of separation, just another "false truth" to which humans have become accustomed.

To free oneself from all limitations also means to let go of the notion of energy. Yes, there is an agreement on how the beings of Earth connect scene spheres by sticking to the notion of energy – after all, it is only through this that common experiences become possible. But you are gradually becoming fully aware *that you are no longer bound by this agreement!*

We can therefore now formulate the role of the dragons more precisely:

Dragons highlight scene spheres!

Alternatively one could say, *dragons highlight potentials!*

Seen from *within* separation, a dragon *seems* to guide energy. Seen from *without*, a dragon highlights potentials that a being can experience according to its beliefs and the agreed upon laws of physics.

The more you free yourself from your beliefs about energy and linear time, the more the dragons are free to brighten scene spheres accessible to you that are far beyond the "normal." It is then up to you whether you want to experience them. Those spheres will not be newly created either, but it might be interesting for you to experience them. And who knows, they may even lead you to the experience of true wisdom.

Ah, by the way, if there is no energy, *then there is certainly no matter either.* The stuff dreams are made of is simply intentions within pure consciousness. Tell that to your big toe next time it hits a rock.

I am Althar, a master of the one and only game having no rule at all.

4. The Unborn Goddess of Feminine Beingness

I am Althar, the Crystal Dragon!

Now I have the honor to introduce one of our guests. Her name is "Ila," pronounced as "Ea-lah" like in *eagle*. You have probably noticed that I always use the male form whenever grammar requires a choice. The reason for this is simply that for historical reasons, the male form is generic as opposed to the female form. But with Ila, I have no choice but to use the female form, even though *Ila has never entered the worlds of separation* and is thus far beyond polarity.

Any expression you could use to describe Ila is inadequate from the start. But in an attempt to somehow indicate her radiance with words, I call her "The Unborn Goddess of Feminine Beingness." It is best not to imagine Ila as an entity, but rather as a "living quality."

Since Ila was never within separation, she has never taken on a body, especially not a physical one. Therefore, to a human consciousness, she appears to be totally *pure and untarnished* in the best sense of the word.

Ila has heard of separation, but for her it is just an unnatural idea. Yet she is always there for those who explore separation. Just as an empathic person simply *knows* when someone else experiences an intense dream, so does Ila. For that, the content of the dream does not need to be known. Ila is simply there and soothes those who dream of separation. In doing so, she does not follow any personal agenda, it is simply in her nature.

One could say that Ila corresponds to a part of you, dear reader, that also never entered the dream of separation. In a way, she represents that *unborn* part of you. She symbolizes your feminine beingness, which *can always give birth to ever-new beingness beyond separation*. Ila thus brings forth *true creation,* just as you can do once you have let go of separation.

*

Any true self entering separation must *necessarily have an imbalance towards the masculine.* There is no other way! Those who want to experience separation or even incarnate must *apply* separation themselves. In other words: *They must fight for survival!*

No matter how much you try to gloss over your human life or try to be peaceful, you cannot survive a single second without destroying the lives of others – be it even the microbes in your belly. Even if it's despised or not done consciously, well, your body will continue to fight off all invaders, for it wants to *survive*. After all, the body is *the* symbol of separation.

So, whether you are inhabiting a male or female body, you are inherently imbalanced, and there is *no way to become balanced while holding on to separation!*

*

Ila will most certainly *not* join you in the dream of separation, but whenever you open up beyond separation you can become aware of her.

You might say that Ila bid you farewell when you set off on the adventure called separation. But she also knows that you never truly left – for where do you go when you daydream?

Ila is also known as the "Goddess of Bliss," because when *you become aware of her as yourself*, all phenomena come to an end and only your pure beingness in bliss remains.

From now on, Ila will be very present. In the next chapters, we will cross a difficult territory and it will be greatly beneficial to know Ila is by our side. Therefore, it would be very helpful if you would open up to Ila for the rest of the day, so that tomorrow you are ready for the Lord of Death.

I am Althar, a blissful dragon.

5. The Lord of Death

I am Aouwa, a true self in expression.

Why, oh why does it seem to be impossible for a human to maintain the state of enlightenment *permanently?* Why does he always return to the limitations of the human mode, even if he has just experienced a longer period of sublime bliss in transcendence?

Well, dear reader, the time has finally come to approach one of the greatest fears that you as a human being carry within you, which contributes significantly to this return effect. You are probably not aware of this fear, although it plays a constant and prominent role in the physics of incarnation, and thus also in the transition from the physical incarnation into the light body.

We have already discussed many things that bind you to the physical dream world. For example, we have discussed patterns and blueprints, be they obvious or hidden. We have explored the core human intentions of time, space, and veiling. Of course, we have dealt extensively with false identities and their interplay with the emotional body and the mind.

So you might think all these ingredients would be enough to make you seriously believe that *you are a body!* A body that is located somewhere in space and bound to a linear stream of time as a separate entity. Consequently, one might also think dissolving all these ingredients should lead to permanent enlightenment and freedom from the physical.

However, as you probably have experienced, this is *not* the case. Why? Because there is something else that plays an essential role that is very, very deeply anchored. One could say we first had to address and solve the mechanisms at the higher levels before we could now approach the following topic in a meaningful way.

If we had talked about this too soon, you might have rejected our remarks or taken them lightly. Or, you could have misused them to set yourself up in a cozy role as the victim of the big picture. But now, after all the discussions we've had, after all the knowledge you've gained, after all the letting go, after all the cultivating of your awareness and your light body – the time has come to face this profound issue.

What we are going to deal with in this and the following chapters will touch very sensitive areas, and it will be very important to truly face them. However, there are many ways to deny or avoid, over and over again, horrible experiences and deep-seated fears as well as feelings of guilt and shame. For example, by pretending to be cool or above the subject, or by rushing past them while reading.

It is therefore certainly not a question of reading the following text as quickly as possible. On the contrary, I encourage you to proceed *very slowly* and take *several pauses* within the chapters. Please use each of the pauses to feel what I am trying to convey beyond words and metaphors.

What we will discuss is not intended to fuel mental discussions with yourself or with others. Rather, it is for *you!* It is for the *deepest part* of you. It is for that part of you *that is chained to the world of matter* and has volunteered to forget everything and everyone and even to separate from the more conscious part of the incarnated morsel of consciousness of your true self.

*

Remember our discussion about the standstill that so many true selves have felt. The standstill represents the insight that within separation there is no true creation, but only repetitions of ever-the-same experiences and story lines. This is the main characteristic of *existence in separation*, also called the Second Round of Creation.

Among the many true selves who became aware of the standstill were I, Aouwa, and most probably your true self, dear reader. So, as already discussed, we came to the decision to try to gain a deeper understanding of creation and hopefully overcome the standstill by way of incarnating.

But with this we faced an incredible challenge: How could we reconcile consciousness and physical matter? Just like fire and water, consciousness and matter simply do not fit together. What could be done to even make the consciousness of an entity believe that *it is a physical form?* This problem was indeed even more difficult to solve than how to create autonomous forms from matter, today known as "biological lifeforms."

At that time, we already knew about the power of beliefs and that they transform the perceptions of an entity into its personal realities. We had hoped that this approach might help us.

However, experiments showed that the introduction of beliefs into an entity was not sufficient to maintain a state of *identification with matter* over a longer period of time. In other words, it was too easy to overcome these beliefs and let go of the illusion of "being of matter." So although the idea of incarnation itself was brilliant, the true selves were at a loss as to how it could be implemented.

At this point, one group came forward and agreed to reveal their deep insights into a technique they thought would solve the problem. The technique consisted of two steps, namely a *compression of consciousness* followed by a kind of *hypnosis* at the deepest possible level.

*

Why was the compression necessary? Figuratively speaking, the vibration of the consciousness that was about to incarnate had to be lowered in order to come as close as possible to the vibration of physical matter. This step of the technique was already extremely challenging, as I will try to describe now.

Imagine the nucleus of an atom. Your scientists have discovered a number of building blocks that are becoming fuzzier and less tangible the smaller the order of magnitude they are studying becomes. Finally, they reach a level where only vague, abstract forces perform a dance in probabilities. Only when scaling upward to the macro level do these abstract forces magically constitute your world of form and perception.

For the sake of our discussion, it suffices to have a metaphorical image of an atom. Let's say that the nucleus of an atom consists of protons and neutrons, which can be imagined as tiny spheres. The important point here is the following: *These spheres cling to each other!* They are so strongly connected that a huge amount of energy is released as soon as they are separated.

Just tear apart a handful of atoms and you have an *atomic explosion.* This is what happens with the so-called atomic bombs. The force of the explosion corresponds to the force with which the protons and neutrons clung together. *Such* are the energies we are dealing with here. These enormous energies are literally bound in *compressed form* in the subatomic structures. These are the building blocks which constitute the world of form. *And into these structures we wanted to inject consciousness!*

To get a feeling for what compression means, consider a real atomic explosion. You have certainly seen the mushroom cloud of an atomic explosion. Such a large phenomenon, emanating from such a tiny source. Imagine you were this mushroom cloud, but now you wanted to contract and return to the source of the explosion. You wanted to *compress* yourself back into a few pounds of atoms.

Compression can therefore be regarded as a *consciousness implosion* that is equal in its force to an *atomic explosion.* In a way, this is exactly what is required to lower the vibration of consciousness close enough to the vibration of the physical plane. In fact, to stay in the picture, it takes not just one, but *a whole series* of reverse atomic explosions. As you may imagine, this is certainly not a pleasant process for the affected consciousness.

As the compression should not go all the way down to the physical, an additional *hypnosis* was required. The *overwhelming desire* to bind with the physical *at the atomic level* had to be anchored in the already low vibrating consciousness. This hypnosis would ensure that the low vibrating consciousness would sooner or later find a way to make itself believe it *was a physical body.*

And it worked! It took a while, but as the low vibrating entities became so connected to the animal life forms that they eventually became part of the cycle of physical birth and death, *the hypnosis struck completely!*

Driven by the hypnosis, a part of the compressed consciousness connected during fertilization with the atomic level of the DNA of the new biological being. With each replication of the DNA, this connection was also passed on to the new cells, so that the consciousness woven into the matter finally had the "natural" feeling of *being a body*. From then on, it was chained not only to the body, but also to the cycle of birth and death.

Does that sound cruel? Yes, it does. But we all knew it would be like this. And you knew it too.

*

The group that had the knowledge of how to compress and hypnotize the consciousness of an entity had hesitated for a while before talking about it. The members of the group knew that they would have a huge price to pay if they revealed their insights. But as they also knew that the looming standstill was very real and that the misperception of their role would only be temporary, they eventually decided to make their knowledge available. They put themselves in service to the common dream of embodied ascension.

This group of experts is known as "Uru" – and even hearing the name could trigger discomfort, fear, and even panic within you. Because of what Uru did with the compression and hypnosis, they were perceived as a demonic monster. Uru became the bogeyman, the Black Man, because they brought absolute darkness over you. Uru is the intangible spook on which you project your fear of pain and death. Uru is the creature that lurks in the dark corners of your cellar. Uru is the abyss that wants to devour you. Uru haunts you in your darkest dreams, threatening to suck your life and your very soul out of you.

And weighting the heaviest of all: Uru represents your horror at being *found guilty* and then damned and imprisoned for eternity. *For eternity!*

*

Uru was the last seen before you departed on your journey into incarnation. Figuratively speaking, Uru locked the door behind you, then sealed and hid it. As soon as that door was closed, the compression began. This was a very unpleasant process that a human would describe as extremely painful and accompanied by choking sensations. You also felt more and more limited by the increased density. Have you ever tried running under water? Well, then try running while Mount Everest is resting on you – so crushing was this feeling of being exposed to the enormous density.

As I will explain in detail in a later chapter, a side effect of the compression was a *veiling* of consciousness. In short, with increasing density, consciousness loses more and more of its natural ability to be aware of its true self.

When you felt this ever-increasing veiling of your consciousness, when you were exposed to this almost unbearable compression, when you felt fear and pain in an intensity completely unknown to you – a thought arose in you:

"I must have done something terrible!"

Why else would you have to endure something like that? Your deed must have been so terrible that it led to this equally terrible treatment. Deep feelings of guilt and shame arose within you, although you couldn't remember what you might have done wrong. *And these feelings of guilt and shame were imprinted directly into the core of your now compressed consciousness.*

When the compression was completed, Uru applied the hypnosis on some *part* of your compressed consciousness. This hypnosis forced you *to want to be physical*. Uru was working on a level of consciousness far below that of beliefs. A plane so subtle that it could be equated with the subatomic particles and abstract forces that make up physical matter. In a way, the hypnosis made part of you extremely magnetized, so that it wanted to connect with its counterpart, the subatomic particles.

And what's more, the hypnosis was *not reversible* by any entity *other than the hypnotized entity itself!* This was a crucial condition for the whole mission. Otherwise, it would have been very likely that groups or individual entities would have abused this knowledge – as has continually happened since the beginning of the Second Round of Creation.

After the entire treatment, you completely forgot who you were. You had no memory that you had voluntarily separated from your true self. The very concept of a true self had been squeezed out of you. The only thing that remained was a vague memory of Uru; of the one who had locked you away and who from then on, symbolized the hangman, prison guard, and torturer.

Even though you may have suppressed any conscious memory of Uru, the side effects of the compression, namely fear, guilt, and shame, are *very real.*

So, is it any wonder that Uru represents *eternal damnation* for so many humans?

And who would want to meet an entity again that is capable of squeezing your very soul out of your being?

Who would even want to come *close* to such an entity?

Who would be so bold as to approach his most innate guilt and shame, knowing that Uru lurks right behind it? And Uru would certainly have further appropriate treatment in store if you tried to escape from your prison of corporeality, wouldn't he?

So, better to turn away and run as soon as a vague remembrance of Uru and what he represents rises up in you.

Better to not meet the guilt and shame within *at all!*

Better to pretend not to carry any guilt or shame whatsoever, to be okay, to be oh-so enlightened and divine, and to only be stuck in the physical with just a tiny fraction of your beingness.

Better to turn to distraction, and hope, and the future.

Better to stay in your human environment where you've been so long. At least, in the mean time you are used to your prison, to your limitations, and to your pain. And who knows what Uru would do to you *if you dared come close to the invisible door?*

Take some time to put yourself into what has happened. Be courageous and allow all memories and fears to emerge.

*

Such were the effects of the compression and hypnosis. Fear, guilt, and shame do not only exist on the higher levels of your consciousness, but they also exist in the portion of your consciousness that is so tightly connected to the physical that it can be considered to be split-off from the rest of your human consciousness. And down there, on this super-unconscious level, these imprints have a tremendous impact. Here resides the greatest attachment and the greatest fear of letting go. Why?

Because releasing the physical triggers the fear of encountering Uru.

But before you could even come close to this fear, you must first overcome layers of guilt and shame. For how could you face your deepest fear of Uru when your self-worth is like a heap of rubble and you have neither self-confidence nor dignity?

But guilt and shame are often suppressed and not directly recognizable as such. Instead, they are projected outward and through mirroring, constantly intensify the more or less subtle feeling of lack of self-worth. And this is exactly how they preserve themselves.

That is also why the process of a natural death is extremely difficult and terrifying for so many people! Ask any person who is terminally ill and suffers from severe pain. At the higher levels of consciousness, this person really wants to leave, but deep down something is holding them back.

Just as connecting consciousness and matter within the framework of incarnation was a monumental challenge, dissolving this connection within the framework of embodied ascension is tremendously difficult – for that was the prerequisite for realizing our vision.

Even though the above may sound a bit dramatic, it is *very* real.

*

Isn't it kind of a cosmic joke that the forces on the micro level are so much more potent than on the macro level? What force can you apply with a muscle? Yet, the very atoms the muscle is made of contain the energy of an atomic bomb.

The same applies to consciousness. You can restructure, ennoble, or let go of thoughts. You can master emotions and feelings, dissolve patterns, and unravel perceptions. But all this takes place on the macro level, on the level of "muscles." But deep inside, on the micro level, lies *the true power that binds you to the physical!*

Another cosmic joke is the following fact: For separation to appear as real as possible, it is necessary that you, as a non-physical consciousness, *believe* that you are physical and *do not want to separate* from matter.

One might even assume that separation is an entity in itself, like the devil, planning and scheming to keep you limited and separated. But don't even think that this was the case. Otherwise, you would be placing yourself under the rule of some entity you consider to be greater than yourself. Instead, just see things as they are:

There is exactly one cause that keeps the wheels of the Second Round of Creation spinning. And of course, you do know what that cause is. It is the firm belief in separation.

And it is your belief in separation that constantly whispers to you through the veil of fear, guilt and shame with a demonic voice on all levels of your being:

"Believe in me! Do not question me! Do not let go of me! For if you do, you will have to endure something like an atomic explosion again. But this time you would tear apart consciousness, which is much stronger and more dangerous than just destroying a few atoms. And then your guilt and shame, which you rightly carry within you, will shatter you. So, my friend, *you better believe in me!* You better hold on to being a separate entity in an isolated body. You better keep pretending to be able to restore divine bliss by shuffling around a few building blocks and thoughts made of separation. This is what you have been doing for eons, and this is what you should continue to do, *unless you want to meet Uru and be extinguished!*"

*

Can you see how the whole setup of incarnating into a human body mimics the occurrence of the thought of separation within pure consciousness?

The fear, guilt, and shame experienced by the compressed portion of your consciousness resembles the fear, guilt, and shame that arose in your true self when it decided to experience separation.

And this is precisely the reason why a human who realizes throughout his whole spectrum of consciousness, down to the deepest core of the physical, *that separation is an illusion, will free his true self from that very illusion!*

Thus, by seeing separation for what it really is, fear, guilt, and shame are completely erased, *because they have no basis!*

Realize that everything that happened in the Second Round of Creation was in a way predetermined. Not in the sense of a destiny determined by a higher deity, but in the sense that *all scene spheres already existed, completely independent of your choices!* You have only traversed and experienced sequences of these already existing spheres. *But no single sequence is better or worse than any other!* Thus, fear, guilt, and shame *only exist within the dream of separation and only as long as you make them real!*

Moreover, since the *entirety* of the scene spheres came into being instantly with the pondering of separation, there is *neither the need nor the possibility to clean up behind you!*

Can you accept it to be that easy?

*

Apparently, within separation there is often a need for the good guy and the bad guy. In our case, when it was about melding consciousness and matter, the good guy was Gaia. She immersed herself into that rock called Earth and brought life force energy in. She nurtured the organisms and creatures.

Is anybody *afraid* of Gaia? Of "Mother Earth?" Not really. She is worshipped, celebrated, appreciated, and all the rest of that. But Gaia alone would simply not have been sufficient for the experiment of incarnation. It probably also needed a bad guy to make it happen.

Uru volunteered to take on the role of the bad guy. He became the hangman, even the "Lord of Death." Kind of funny, isn't it? The *real* Lord of Death is obviously *you*, who still clings to the belief in separation. For how could there even *be* death without separation? You are simply your own, very personal Lord of Death!

So Uru's task was to compress you and to hypnotize you, such that you eventually *believed yourself to be a physical body*. And even when the body you incarnated into died, *you still carried that hypnotic implant with you!* So not only did you yearn for new incarnations at the higher levels of your consciousness, but the micro level of your consciousness was *craving* them.

All of this was part of the plan we came up with to overcome the standstill.

And it was Uru who enabled all of us to succeed.

It was Uru who made life in flesh and blood possible.

It was Uru who provided the knowledge and skills to realize incarnation and ascension as a human on Earth.

It is time to see Uru as what he truly is and to honor his service.

It is time, dear reader, to let go of the fear of Uru – for you will meet him again as soon as you have faced your deepest layers of guilt and shame.

And by the way, *this is exactly why the dragons came back!* They came to help you clean your house, so to speak. They support you in dissolving false identities, they point out limiting imprints, they bring all kinds of guilt and shame to light. When you are eventually able to meet the dragon and recognize him as what he really is, then Uru will look like the old friend he really always was.

*

For the moment, we will leave it at that. Please take some time to feel deeply into all levels of what we have just discussed. I strongly advise you not to read on until tomorrow. Allow yourself a night of deep sleep before continuing. Allow yourself to slowly prepare to face your deepest fear.

I am Aouwa.

6. Micro Level Bindings of Consciousness

I am Althar, the Crystal Dragon!

Most of the discussions we've had so far worked on the macro level of consciousness. We dealt with concepts such as patterns, beliefs, perceptions, and core intentions. Now we want to take a deeper look at the effects of Uru's compression and hypnosis so we are going down to the micro level of consciousness.

Uru compressed a part of the consciousness of your true self so much that it has become denser and denser. This did not only lead to the feelings of fear, guilt, and shame described above, but the compressed consciousness also became extremely *dull* and *unaware*.

This state, heavily dazed and strongly condensed, is already very close to being physical matter. But now, Uru additionally wove a hypnosis into this already compressed consciousness, which led to the overwhelming desire to *bind* to the physical at the subatomic level especially at the level of the genome, the DNA. Once the hypnosis came to fruition, the hypnotized consciousness attached itself to the particles constituting the DNA *with the same intensity* as the protons and neutrons that cling to each other.

Recognize that this actually resulted in a "double split-off." Through the compression, a morsel of the true self's consciousness is split-off from its true self. As a result, *this part is initially totally unaware of its very own origin.* Then, through the hypnosis, a portion of the already compressed consciousness is split-off *so it could bind to matter.* By binding to matter, the incarnated consciousness now has the overwhelming impression of being *in and out of physical matter.* So although consciousness is not matter at all, part of it is now so strongly magnetized and bound to the physical that the *impression of existing in matter as matter feels overwhelmingly real.*

In other words, a part of the consciousness is now so deeply and firmly convinced that it is matter, that one can speak of "incarnation" – the becoming of flesh.

However, a split-off of consciousness can *never really* take place! It is only played out in the dream of separation. In fact, the consciousness remains *internally united.*

Thus, even if your human macro level consciousness can open far into the non-physical realms, the hypnosis of your micro level ensures that you are always pulled back to your physical body.

*

Psychologists use the term "the unconscious" to describe a level of consciousness that significantly influences a person's feelings and actions. Although the psychologists are usually, well, unconscious about the effects of the micro level bindings, the term itself is very appropriate.

As the impulses coming from the unconscious are by their very definition below the conscious awareness of the human, these impulses are, quite frankly, often times a pain in the ass. Even though you have gained wisdom and insight, and even though you have let go of many obvious and some obstinate patterns, there still seems to be something lingering inside you that *makes you act against your own best interests!*

As always, the most important step in solving a problem is to become clear about what is actually going on. Thus, the fact that you now *know* about the hypnosis is an essential step in its removal.

Let's also take a closer look at some of the effects of the bindings at the micro level. For the sake of discussion, let us assume that physical manifestations are structured from lesser to more complex formations. So, we have subatomic particles, atoms and then molecules. From there we go on into biological structures and have single-celled organisms, multi-celled organisms, tissues, organs, and finally the body of a human being.

The split-off part of consciousness hypnotized into matter follows this increasing complexity. It always assumes that it *is* the structure on the respective level and adopts its specific characteristics.

At the atomic and molecular level, it only *wants to bind strongly to the particles and atoms.* However, on a cellular level, it wants to *survive as a cell.* A cell does not philosophize about its existence and does not complain about it. It only wants to survive as a cell and produce offspring. It does everything to achieve exactly that – and this is what the physically bound consciousness takes on at the cellular level and therefore, *also wants*. It does not want to let go of its "cell-ness" at any price, because letting go of this identification means death, and that would be completely against the prevailing will to survive. The very same happens on all higher levels of complexity.

Therefore, as soon as you, dear reader, prepare at the macro level to let go of the physical, every atom of your body, every molecule, every cell, and every organ will *loudly and sustainably* object to it:

"Let go? Crazy, or what?!"

*

On a macro level, you are very aware of the human mass consciousness and how it affects you. Unfortunately, it is by no means easy to get rid of it. It is as if you wanted to swim naked in the ocean without getting wet. Sure, when you wake up from the dream of separation, you will realize that you don't have a body at all, so you don't have to worry about wetness. But prior to that, you will not escape the wetness of the ocean.

You need an enormous awareness not to be too influenced by the human mass consciousness that is all around you. Of course, the easiest way to achieve this is to avoid it as much as possible.

You can choose not to read or watch the news anymore, and you can minimize your encounters with larger groups of people. But as sensitive as you are, you always feel this buzzing of mass consciousness with all its fears and desires, and sometimes, as you know, it just sweeps you away.

The point I want to make is this: *The human body with all of its cells is very similar to the human mass consciousness!*

Your body consists of approximately 10^{14} cells, so there are about 100,000 times more cells in your body than there are humans on the planet. All of these cells constantly communicate with each other and with their lower structures. And they talk about nothing but s*urvival, food, and reproduction.*

You are so used to this permanent buzzing of your mass of cells and organs that it goes unnoticed – unless you are about to detach yourself from the physical. Then, your inner being screams out loud in the form of instincts and drives to dissuade you! At first, it tries utilizing emotions and fears, but if that doesn't work, the body simply denies your macro consciousness cooperation.

You want to know what that feels like? Well, take a deep breath, then hold your breath and *slowly* count to hundred.

*

Let's be honest, you barely manage to *move* your body and hack into its sensory perceptions!

But you have virtually no influence on any other bodily functions – and when the linear mind tries, it usually only causes confusion.

So, if you go with your macro consciousness on a journey into the higher realms of existence, then it is as if your consciousness is pulled apart. One part is becoming "lighter" while another is still woven into the physical body structures. And the latter part *does not want to let go!* It has been hypnotized to believe *it is physical!* For that part, letting go *equals death and extinction!*

Thus, when you move too far or for too long away from the physical, the micro level of consciousness starts sending out signals like fear, strong hunger, or overwhelming sexual desire. At first discreet, then stronger and stronger, until finally, it just takes over and *pulls you back!*

The micro level is so strong because it consists of an unimaginable number of cells and atoms *working against your choice on the macro level.* Moreover, the only reason that you have survived so long at all is because *you learned to obey these signals!*

Have you ever wondered about why "going out there" made you so incredibly hungry that you literally had to stuff yourself afterwards? Be it with food, water, alcohol, or sex? Well, that was to *calm your unconscious.* That was to sink yourself *back into the physical.* That was to make your unconscious feel *safe* again.

As if that weren't enough, there's even more to it. Your personal mass consciousness does not only originate from your current incarnation! There is a bleed-through of all your incarnations and life forms that are actually taking place right now. And the more conscious you become, the more you become aware of these other influences. In other words, if you are about to let go of the belief in separation on behalf of your true self, you will encounter not only the resistance of your own body and human consciousness, *but also the resistance of all these other incarnations and life forms!*

Pretty huge, eh?

Yes, it is annoying. Yes, it is not that easy to overcome. But hey, *that was part of the deal!* That was the price you had to pay so you could experience physical creation from within as a seemingly physical being and eventually realize enlightenment on behalf of your true self and all of existence! So, hero, just stop complaining and let's see how your situation can be undone by not-doing anything.

*

Even if it looks like you are really in a jam, isn't consciousness a great thing? I mean, briefly consider my perspective: Even if consciousness is limited by separation, it produces an amazingly complex, intricate, interdependent, self-reinforcing, seductive, and ultimately elegant experience. From the outside, this is truly *phenomenal* – in the truest sense of the word.

Good. Back to you, dear friend. What can we not-do to assist you?

Before we discuss this in a later chapter, I would first like you to become aware of the *strength* and *uncompromising nature* of the part of your consciousness that has been hypnotized into the physical and its structures. To do so, we will spend some time drawing your attention to your weakly covered animal and cellular nature. Why? *Because they will reappear as soon as you try to release the bonds on the micro level!* Thus, it's best to be aware of them so you are not over-whelmed by some archaic faces of yourself.

Even if all of this seems to be insurmountable, always remember that at your core *you are pure consciousness*. In a way, *you* have created all of this and it takes much more effort to keep it up and running than to clean it up.

I am Althar, C4, Certified Cosmic Cleansing Coach.

7. Let's Talk Blood

I am Althar, the Crystal Dragon!

In the previous chapter, we have talked in a more abstract way of what the micro level bindings of consciousness and their letting go imply. Now is the time to get more sensual and to explicitly draw your attention to some of the experiences you might have when letting go of the physical plane. This is especially important in the context of the light body exercise, which we will examine once again shortly. Therefore:

Let's talk blood!

Feel into your animal nature, into your existence as a predator that still lingers deep inside you. Specifically, I ask you to *become a saber-toothed tiger! Now!*

*

Ah, the saber-toothed tiger – such an archaic and impressive creature. Can you feel your raw *power*? Your *instincts*? The *grace* in your body movements? Can you feel what it's like to *hunt* down your prey? To bite into its throat and taste the blood? *Sure you can!* After all, it wasn't that long ago, was it? Allow yourself to feel it again! Oh, it wasn't just about feeding, it was also about the feeling of *devouring the life energy of another being!*

Take some time and immerse yourself once more in these experiences. Go hunt! Taste the sweet victory! *Drink blood!*

*

These experiences as an animal at the top of the food chain gave you the feeling of raw physical power. They were neither good nor bad. They were *intense!* Sure, sooner or later *you* were the one eaten, but that was only fair and part of the game – at least it felt better than slowly wasting away and dying of old age.

Due to their intensity, these experiences of raw physical power were reflected in the DNA and blueprints of animal organisms. So, whether or not *you* have ever inhabited a saber-toothed tiger, these memories are a part of the biology of your body and the common reservoir of memories. They are raw, pure and intense. To this day, *they are a part of you* and slumber right behind the human facade!

In the course of the evolution of human consciousness, you have learned to tame your animal instincts through denial and oppression. You also replaced them with something less bloody. Nowadays, most humans no longer kill with bites, but with *thoughts, emotions, and words.*

In a sense, this is a cheap substitute for the good old days, but it allowed you to survive long enough for your consciousness to strive for enlightenment and enter the realm of non-separation. But since you are still bound to the physical, the struggle for survival and the thirst for blood are *still deeply imprinted in you.*

Let us now come to the other end of the spectrum of physical bodies, a single-celled organism. A few billion of them are bustling right now inside your mouth. Choose one of those cells and *immerse yourself in it.* Feel it from within. How is it to exist as a single-celled organism?

*

A cell receives only a few sensory impressions and is based on comparatively simple stimulus-response schemes. Nevertheless, it has an awareness of self-existence, and it wants one thing above all: *It wants to survive.*

Can you feel that? Can you feel your consciousness being bound to a single cell and blind to almost everything that is going on around it? It is only about survival. And in order to survive, you have to *feed, reproduce, and fight.*

Stay as a single-celled organism for a few moments.

*

The behavioral patterns that ensure survival are deeply rooted in the DNA of each individual cell. From there they continue into the more complex structures such as tissues, organs, and finally the whole organism. The desire to survive is passed on *to each level* and is expressed there accordingly.

Now, feel this whole conglomerate. Feel the constant stimulus-response chains at the cellular level, which are always striving to ensure survival. Then, the raw feelings of power at the level of the predator. The *taste of survival* in the form of warm blood, running down your throat after a good fight.

Your hypnotized consciousness is *identified with these impulses, drives, and experiences*, and this part of your consciousness continues to want on all levels of its hypnotized existence *what it has always wanted – survival!*

As you slowly reverse the hypnosis by cultivating your light body, all these old patterns are literally washed out of your DNA. Thereby, they are activated, exposing you to a whirlpool of instincts, drives, stimulus-response schemes, traumas, and repressive mechanisms that rise from the unconscious into your awareness.

You may also suddenly feel that you have an excess of energy, just like a predator at the height of its physical power. So you want to run and hunt down prey. But prey can also just be the "next big project" you use to experience your strength – and in which you get so entangled that all your noble desires to let go are suffocated. Once again!

*

Letting go *must* proceed from the higher levels of consciousness to the lower, for nothing would be gained if you let go of your physical body, only to take with you all sorts of mind confusion into the non-physical realms. Well, this is what happens with the physical death of every ordinary person, but that's not our subject right now.

By now, you have resolved many, if not most, of the challenges that reside on the macro level of human consciousness, such as your false identities. That was difficult enough already, but, quite frankly, it's downright peanuts compared to what awaits you at the micro level, because there your hypnotized consciousness believes it is *about bare survival.*

Let's take two examples of what you can do in such a moment. Once again, put yourself in a saber-toothed tiger at the height of his physical power after a recent kill. He is wounded himself, but still the blood and flesh of his prey provide an overwhelming satisfaction. See it! Feel it! *Be it!*

Then, remind yourself that *this is all but a dream!* And now is the time to *wake up!* All this *is not real* and it *was never real!* Let this tiger dissolve into the bliss of pure awareness. *Now!*

And further, feel a single cell that exists in an unknown void. *Be this cell!* Then become aware *as this cell* that *all this is just a dream! Wake up! Now!*

Remember these remarks whenever the impulses of the micro level threaten to sweep you away. Remember it *especially* when you feel surges of power arise in you and you want to tear down trees, turn the world upside down, or just go hunting.

*

Should we have talked earlier about this? Surely not, for it would have been of no help. But now it is important that you realize what is really going on. You are in the in-between zone. Everything that you thought was reality dissolves more and more with your letting go. You are now beginning to release the parts of your consciousness from the dream of separation that are so deeply woven into matter that you were convinced *you were a body.*

If you had decided to leave your body with your enlightenment, you would not have had to worry about such things. But since you intend to stay, you have to face all this.

The insights that have just been given will be very helpful when cultivating your light body. You will experience again and again variants of fear and raw power, which you do not know from your human experiences. At the cellular level, each cell will release its DNA-based fear, which is associated with the belief in separation and the fear of extinction. It will also release the imprinted guilt and shame and flood you with feelings of overwhelming inferiority. Inferior, because you did not even know who you were anymore, and obviously had done something so dreadful that you were condemned to a life in matter. On the animalistic level, instincts want to be lived out again.

But now you know the game. Now you know the ways of polarity. So do not be fooled! Be the eye of the storm. Let the emotions and anxiety, the instincts for survival, and the raw impulses all swirl around you. *They are not real!*

Dear friend, the time of blood is already over, just like the Second Round of Creation. Leave it be. Just leave it be. *None of this has ever been real in the first place.*

I am Althar, the peacemaker.

8. Blueprints and DNA

I am Althar, the Crystal Dragon!

Now that we have talked about the binding of incarnated consciousness to DNA, we want to look more closely at the DNA and the more general principle of blueprints. Then it will become very clear that letting go of the DNA and the blueprints means nothing less than *the end of existing as a self as you know it!*

DNA is the physical equivalent of non-physical blueprints. The origins of blueprints go back to the very first beginnings of the exploration of separation, long before physical matter came into play. When the true selves entered separation, they did not know who, where, or what they were. They felt deeply *unsafe*. However, they realized at some point that by *repeatedly experiencing* the same intentions, they could create some kind of *stability*. By doing so, at least a sentiment of relative safety arose, since surprises were less frequent due to the constant repetitions.

Put yourself in your true self and imagine what it was like to have no idea who, what, or where you are. But then, *by repeating experiences,* you gradually created the first stable reflection of yourself. It felt very pleasant, but at the same time you have also shaped *your first false identity!*

The arrangement of intentions according to the desire to experience repetitions finally crystallized into what we now call blueprints. Blueprints define the core attributes of any species, whether non-physical or physical. Only by having their experiences based on the same or similar blueprints can entities relate to each other and share common experiences.

The differences between the various spiritual families are due to the *different blueprints* followed by the respective family members. Birds of a feather flock together, and when several entities share the same beliefs, they feel all the more confirmed in them.

Human DNA is thus the physically visible counterpart to the non-physical human blueprint. It contains layers upon layers of patterns and information, both physical and non-physical.

It is the DNA that forms the biological body with its general and personal characteristics. It is the DNA that defines the framework of potential experiences. It is the DNA that transmits imprints and traumas that originate at the level of species, biological lineage, or present life. It is the DNA into which the incarnating consciousness is woven and which becomes its prison. It is the DNA that the hypnotized consciousness constantly believes is whispering: *"Hold on to me or you will disappear from existence!"*

Something very similar takes place on the level of the true self. Just as it is almost impossible for a human to let go of his DNA and thus his physicality, it is almost impossible for a true self to let go of the blueprints it has created or adopted, and the false identity that goes with them. But holding on to blueprints of whatever kind is nothing other than maintaining limitations. In other words:

Holding on to blueprints corresponds to holding on to the belief that separation is real!

*

I have already briefly addressed the blueprints in previous messages and mentioned the impact of embodied ascension on them. The vision of embodied ascension certainly does not culminate in experiencing tremendous fun in the physical, or in finally being the brilliant and successful person you may have always wanted to be. After all, how long can it be fulfilling to be a star in kindergarten? And if there is no more feeling of lack, how satisfying can abundance be? For some time, you will enjoy it, but you will quickly realize that this alone is no reason to stay on Earth.

The primary vision of embodied ascension was to overcome the standstill – *but that was not all!* The vision behind the vision of embodied ascension is that by staying in the physical, you are helping to *change the blueprints!* This is the meaning of "The first will pave the way!"

The presence of an enlightened person on Earth demonstrates that enlightenment is possible, thereby setting an example for other humans. But when you take on the larger perspective, you realize that with every breath you take as an enlightened being on Earth, *you leave an imprint in the blueprints!*

You will automatically help to *create, stabilize, and highlight* new sections in the human blueprint and DNA! These sections will enable the entities coming after you to make a smoother transition out of polarity into non-separation. It simply doesn't have to remain the case that a human will typically have to experience so much suffering, pain, and grief before he allows himself to let go. In fact:

It is time to heal the Wound of Creation!

This will happen through a kind of healing that does not force anything upon anyone, but that simply makes the simple and natural way beyond separation *shine clearly! This* is the vision behind the vision of embodied ascension!

This is why the light body is so important for those who want to remain "embodied." The light body simplifies the existence within the physical enormously. In addition, your physical body becomes an extension of your light body and can continue to interact with normal people. But the light body itself *is not based on any blueprint* that predetermines all possible characteristics and patterns. Rather, it is a *conscious projection* of a free entity.

However, by you staying in the physical and projecting your light body into physical reality, *a pattern for letting go of polarity is established in the blueprints of humans!* It is like creating a well-lit exit door, a portal shining in beauty through which anyone can go beyond separation.

Note that this pattern is *not* actively fabricated! It is not like you or anyone else is going out into the realm of blueprints and tinkering with some changes. Rather, *it happens naturally as you continue to exist as an enlightened being in separation.*

*

It is also interesting to note that the human blueprint is a *compilation of the blueprints of all existing physical and non-physical species of the entire cosmos!* Why? Because it was decided that by means of the human species the standstill should be overcome *on behalf of all creation.* Thus, the *entire spectrum* of all species and their characteristics had to be represented in the human blueprint.

This is precisely why there are so many humans with completely different dispositions. In their behavior, some seem to resemble reptiles, while others resemble insects, predators, fairies, or dragons. Well, maybe this perspective will help you to accept the "otherness" of the others more easily.

And here's another clue. Your scientists still wonder why so much of human DNA seems so meaningless that they even call it garbage. Well, perhaps these parts of your DNA communicate with other emanations of your true self in other realms of existence and time streams. Perhaps these beings experience a very different version of the same events as you do as a human being.

Maybe there is even a continuous exchange between you, because after all, it is about gaining true wisdom. But that is just a thought.

As interesting and impressive as this background information may be, there are two main points I would like to convey in this chapter. The first is the following:

You are not your DNA!

You are not a molecule, no matter how fascinating it is and how many layers it may have. Also, embodied ascension is not in any way about "upgrading" your body to another dimension or unlocking unused features of your DNA. Sorry, but this is just misleading and confusing esoteric drivel! Why? *Because your true self has already had these experiences!* You have incarnated to *let go of any limitation!* You do *not* want to go backwards – you want to come out at the other end of the tunnel!

Sure, there are entities who take themselves extremely seriously, but have never been incarnated themselves! They might pride themselves on being more technologically advanced than humans. They may want to "help" you *to become like them.* Nice offer. Well, if that is what you desire, no one will stop you from accepting it. But you might also share with them some true wisdom and teach *them* about letting go. *That* would be a nice offer, wouldn't it?

The second essential point is that even *your true self has been holding on to blueprints since time immemorial and thus continues to hold on to separation!*

It could let them go at any time, but so far it has not succeeded completely. As you know, it will be *you* who, through your own final letting go, will flood your true self so much with wisdom that it will literally not be able to hold on to *anything* anymore. Then you will become a beingness that is not comparable with the existence as a limited "self" as you and your true self have ever known before.

I am Althar, definitely crystalline, not blueprinted.

9. The Revelation of True Power

I am Althar, accompanied by the radiance of Ila!

This chapter is about *revelation!* Ah, the word revelation sounds so mysterious, so irresistible. When something is revealed to you, you feel like you're something special. You must have been chosen somehow, right? For how could one reveal *anything* to someone who is not worthy? But now I have even combined the word "revelation" with "power" – and already I am the superstar of the moment. *Yes!*

Well, I admit without any shame that I chose this heading to gain your fullest attention, dear reader. And I can feel...

It worked! Once again! The way it has always worked. Throughout all the eons of existence, revelation has been the *bait par excellence.* Well, nowadays "Wishful thinking" and "Abundance" also work quite well, but I didn't want to go *that* far.

In the end, however, there's not really much to reveal. There is actually only this one thing: "Consciousness is," also known as: "I am that I am." That's it. End of revelation.

But as a human gradually approaches the final realization of this single truth of "consciousness is," he undergoes a deep transformation. He experiences the dissolution of all levels of his imaginary existence, whereby the realization and embodiment of "consciousness is" becomes the most difficult thing a person could ever face.

That is why, often unnoticed, he receives support in many ways. This should encourage him to move forward, not to stop letting go of his beliefs, and to continue his own deconditioning. And that is exactly what something like revelation is best for. It is another stimulus to continue the journey. Our concern, however, is not so much to spur you on, but to prepare you for a challenge that you will not be able to avoid.

We hereby reveal to you that you will have *unimaginable power* in the foreseeable future. Yes, *POWER!* Power which the typical spiritual student claims to have overcome, or worse, which he claims doesn't interest him at all.

What an incredible joke! What a tremendous self-delusion!

Since the separated human strives to recreate his version of pure consciousness' heaven in the physical world, *how could he not strive for power?* Perhaps he calls it persuasiveness, creative will, or assertiveness. Maybe he also tries religion, ethics, or humanism – but I call it by its name:

It is the desire for power!

It is the desire to shape the world according to one's own ideas. But since the "other" usually also has *other* ideas, it is ultimately always the *desire for power over others!* I don't object to that, because within separation, *it can't be any different!*

Take a moment and allow yourself to feel *the seductive beauty of power.* Also consider what true power might have to do with loosening your bindings to matter, DNA, and blueprints.

*

A human typically equates power with being *stronger than* something, or he understands it as the ability to dominate people. This kind of power is based on polarity. It works with the illusion of energy and therefore *reinforces the illusion of separation!*

However, what the human calls "power" is *in its essence* present in pure consciousness as *true power.* Through it, pure consciousness brings forth *true creation!*

Human power is merely the *distorted imitation of true power* inherent in pure consciousness.

If you, dear reader, want to embody pure consciousness, then y*ou cannot reject any of its attributes!* But the closer you get to the true power, *the stronger you inevitably feel its seductive echo* – the human power based on polarity!

Since you consciously or unconsciously remember having abused *human* power in the past, you tend to shy away from *true* power. You doubt that you are ready to deal with it again. You fear that this abundance of power could simply tear you or others apart. So you reject true power, declare your behavior as "spiritually correct" – *and thus hold on to your own limitations!*

So instead of rejecting power, you must be willing to *accept* it!

You must be ready to *embody* power *without succumbing to the temptations of human power!*

Recognize that there is *no power other than your own pure consciousness!*

Realize: You yourself are the true power of creation!

*

I have said over and over again that nothing can withstand pure consciousness. This does not mean that anything in the material realm would be actively changed or even destroyed when exposed to pure consciousness. Rather, it means that in the awareness of your true self, *you have the power not to be disturbed by any phenomenon!* You simply use your inherent power to *be the master of your feelings!*

I call this kind of power the "inner power," because you use it only *within your own being.* Through the inner power, you can also stop following inner impulses. In this way, you gradually withdraw any reality from its originators, be they patterns or false identities, so that they eventually dissolve.

The *inner power* is the only power you can use in polarity that *will not negatively affect you!* It is *passive!* It will not contribute to solidify a false identity that is defined by separation and human power of whatever kind.

So as you approach the *true* power of pure consciousness and the temptations of human power rise within you, transform it into the *inner* power. The inner power will allow you to exist in separation without the phenomena dictating your feelings.

In other words: You simply see with the *Eye of Suchness* – and no phenomenon will be able to withstand your inner power.

Maybe it's time to use *that* kind of power. Maybe it's time to use your inner power to confront those annoying patterns and false identities. Perhaps the time is ripe to put an end to the things you no longer want to tolerate by applying your inner power of pure consciousness.

By using your inner power consciously and continuously, you are no longer restricted by your limited *reactions*. Rather, you can navigate the ocean of scene spheres at will. You literally have the power to choose what you want to experience in separation – and you don't have to create it or use energies for it, because the scene spheres already exist.

The more you open up to your inner power, the greater your ability will be to move freely in separation. With your final letting go, the inner power then transforms into true power, and bringing forth true creation will become your natural expression.

*

I came with Ila for good reason to talk about this topic. For a human, a dragon represents the unrelenting force of existence and thus raw power. Typically, a human is awestruck by the power radiated from a dragon, but tends to get scared or even overwhelmed by it. However, the dragon only reflects the power that *the human pretends not to have!*

Ila, on the other hand, radiates a finer version of power. Ila, just like the power she radiates, is beyond polarity, and *you can feel it.* Ila is in no way threatening, although she has the power of the creation of pure consciousness.

In fact, the term "power" has no meaning to her. Power is one of those concepts that only emerges with the immersion in separation. At Ila's level, it makes no sense to isolate attributes like power, love, or wisdom, because they are naturally united there.

Humans, however, make these distinctions. But while a human striving for enlightenment usually has no problems with love or wisdom, he resists his power – *and thus refuses his completion!*

But if you let go more and more of the physical and come ever-closer to your true nature, *you will inevitably have to face the true power of creation.*

Accept and transform it into inner power that frees you from fixed patterns, rather than into a power of polarity that continues to bind you to separation.

Now take some time and become aware of *your own powerful dragon nature!* At the same time, feel the pure consciousness and the true power of creation as radiated by Ila. Realize that true power has nothing to do with physical energies. Then feel the transformation of true power into inner power. Accept it and *apply it to your inner world!* This is the way to liberation.

*

Your inner world is in no way separated from the outer world. So it is *you*, dear friend, who has all the power you could ever imagine. This goes hand in hand with the responsibility to use it wisely.

Even though this may sound a bit exuberant, it is still the simple truth. If there is any discomfort in you because of the magnitude of your power, well, sorry, but there is no way back – that's just the way it is with revelations.

I am Althar, accompanied by Ila, surfing the true power of creation.

10. The Bearer of the Light

I am Aouwa, a true self in expression!

It is a great honor for me, dear reader, to finally come to this message and deliver it to you. Now that we have waited thousands and thousands of years for the right time and completed all the necessary preparations with our many previous messages, the time has come.

Having to be patient over a long period of time is quite peculiar, even if you're beyond time like me. Waiting seems unbearable, but when the anticipated moment suddenly comes, it seems as if there was no waiting at all. Instead, it's *all about that precious moment.* So, come with me and let's dive right into it.

*

Let us first recapitulate what point we have reached in the meantime. We have seen that through the process of incarnation, your consciousness assumed the firm belief *it was* physical. Furthermore, a deep fear of meeting Uru again arose.

This fear is accompanied by feelings of guilt and shame stemming from the assumption that you must have done something extremely awful. For why else would someone be exposed to this agonizing compression that has transformed you into your present state of being? A state of being that equals eternal damnation.

The feelings of fear, guilt, and shame are not only located on the comparatively easily accessible higher levels of your consciousness, but they are also rooted on the micro level of your consciousness which identifies with your organs, cells, and the subatomic particles of your DNA.

When a "part" of pure consciousness pondered the idea of separation and was literally sucked and fragmented into it, it felt very much the same agony as did the sub part that split off a few eons later when it was compressed into the density of the physical realm.

Metaphorically speaking, *both occurrences were painful and traumatic.* Therefore, both the true self that went off to explore the idea of separation, as well as the consciousness of an incarnated human being that went off to explore life in matter, *carry a very similar burden of fear, guilt and shame.*

Although the human longs so much for completion, the fear of having another experience similar to that of fragmentation or compression prevents him from even approaching the final letting go. Instead of seeing things as they are, he tries to rebuild the perfection of pure consciousness within separation *by regrouping fragments of separation over and over again.*

But since this simply cannot lead to the desired lasting success, he exalts his existence. He claims to be content with *a few moments* of relaxation, beauty, or love. He commits himself to projects and missions, hopes for the future, and glorifies ephemeral phenomena – all in an attempt to give "meaning" to his troublesome existence in separation.

But just as every true self, sooner or later, becomes aware of the ever-recurring same experiences and the lack of true creation within separation, so does the human. After all, the standstill within separation is omnipresent.

So, he sets out to overcome the separation. But no matter which path he chooses, he will eventually encounter the feelings of fear, guilt, and shame that are anchored on the micro level.

And that's where we are right now. Ready to face this greatest challenge. If you, dear reader, were not ready for it, you would certainly not be reading these lines. You would have discarded all these messages long ago, just as you have discarded so many similar representations of the same truth in the past. Remember?

So, how can we deal with the challenges of the micro level? In this message, I will describe the background of what we are proposing. Later, we will see how it integrates into the light body exercise.

*

The most important element in dissolving the bonds at the micro level of consciousness is to fully realize that guilt and shame *have absolutely no basis!* Separation is a *dream*, and nothing that has ever happened in it *has really happened!* In fact, everything you ever did, *you "did" to yourself!* This is true on the macro level as well as on the micro level of consciousness.

Unfortunately, however, this is not a realization that *immediately* frees you from the shackles caused by guilt and shame. Instead, you must always consciously come back to it. You will need to have unlimited, unconditional compassion for yourself again and again as soon as you recognize your patterns of behavior resulting from guilt and shame. And as soon as you recognize them, *you just stop acting them out!* This means to apply the Eye of Suchness unwaveringly, persistently, and boldly.

But besides guilt and shame, there is also the fear of falling into the hands of Uru again. *Uru is very real!* If you have no conscious memories of him, use the name as a symbol for the agonizing compression process that the incarnating consciousness has endured.

Resolving fears and traumas often requires a very personal approach. However, it is *always* very helpful to change the perspective so that the full picture of what ultimately led to the trauma can be seen. Therefore, we will now go into the events of that time in more detail. This will allow Uru to appear in a completely different light, and may help you to better deal with still existing fears.

Uru is not an individual, but a group of entities that form a subbranch of the Uriel family. However, to keep the wording simple, I will sometimes refer to Uru as if it were a single being, but I still always mean the individual members of the group.

Since the beginning of separation, Uru has paid particular attention to exploring the mechanisms underlying the Second Round of Creation. This is why Uru is also called the "Family of Master Scientists."

Just like any entity who ever entered the dream of separation, Uru felt he had lost something. More than any other, Uru wanted to know how he came into the world of separation, and how he could get out of it. Recall that all of us didn't have any notions like separation or polarity back then! We were literally blank pages, but pages having a faint border that separated us from the "others."

Uru was so fascinated by these questions that he was not so attracted by other possible experiences within separation. As a result, he was not so much distracted by having all sorts of experiences and became less entangled in false identities and patterns of all kinds. Therefore, it can be said metaphorically that Uru has remained as close as possible to pure consciousness. This is exactly what makes Uru a part of Uriel's larger family.

Note that I don't make any assessment here. Uru is not somehow "better," because they have kept out of many things and the others are not "worse," because they have burdened themselves with more patterns due to many experiences.

In fact, it is a mystery why an entity at the very beginning of its being in separation has developed one or the other passion. But it was these original passions that eventually led to the formation of spiritual families and corresponding blueprints.

Because of his passion for research, it was only natural that Uru was the first family to discover and realize the "Principle of Ascension." They did this by *applying compression and hypnosis to themselves!*

At that time, however, they did not compress their consciousness to the density of the physical plane, but remained in the non-physical. As a result, the return from compression and hypnosis did not yet unfold the hoped-for depth effect. One could say that the veiling of consciousness was not yet strong enough. So, it was *too easy* to let go of the belief in being separated from the true self. But the results nourished the hope that it might work if compression were continued to the density of the physical plane.

However, Uru was also aware of the possibility that once an entity splits off a part of itself and has incarnated in a physical body, it *might be crippled forever.* Uru was also aware of the fact that the process of compression was very, very agonizing and could cause some ugly side effects – these side effects are the previously mentioned feelings of fear, guilt, and shame. At that time, however, we had no way of predicting them. The necessary hypnosis, on the other hand, while not painful, had extremely serious effects.

Uru explained all this in the assembly that had been discussing how to overcome the standstill. As you can imagine, the description of the process was not exactly tempting. Although it sounded somehow like a great adventure, no entity had gone through anything like that before. And who would dare to expose himself not only to the power of a single explosion, but to a whole series of atomic explosions?

However, when some members of Uru volunteered to be the first to leave, many entities from the other families took courage and joined them. They all became the first wave – and chances are good, dear reader, that you were one of them.

In light of this description of the circumstances, you can now re-evaluate the role played by Uru. Instead of continuing to see him as the Lord of Death, you can recognize him as what he really has always been: *The Bearer of the Light.*

Yes, he compressed and hypnotized a part of your true self into the belief it was physical, and into becoming the human I am speaking to right now. In this part, which is now *you*, he also veiled the last remnants of the light of pure consciousness that your true self still carries within itself even in separation.

But he did it, *because you asked him to!* He enabled you to gain experience and incarnate again and again, until you finally emerge on the other side of the tunnel – *and thus accept and realize your true nature as a sovereign creator being on behalf of your true self!*

Thus, Uru is indeed the *Bearer of the Light* and from the beginning, he's been right with you in the experience of being "human on Earth."

And Uru asks you right now, dear reader, to see the *whole* picture. Even though you remember him as the one who has locked, sealed, and hid the door behind you, *he has simply fulfilled an agreement!*

You volunteered to go through this darkest night of the soul – a journey through the physical – so you could discover, understand, and release the one root cause of the Second Round of Creation: *The belief in separation.*

*

Uru now increases his presence a bit and encourages you to shift your perspective of what has happened. He asks you to release him from what he has never done. As you forgive him for what he has never done, your fear of Uru and what he represents can dissolve.

As you forgive Uru for what he has never done, you also forgive yourself for having been immersed in matter, thereby allowing the last remaining divine spark within you to be veiled.

You realize that even this apparent fall from grace *did not really happen!* As you direct your perspective to the overall picture, guilt and shame can dissolve.

Whenever you approach the final letting go and feel fear coming up, *remember this message!*

Transmute the fear into joy, for you know the final letting go is just a blink away.

Know this: Letting go of the belief in separation will *not* lead to another torment. Instead, *it is the ultimate liberation and the realization of your true nature.*

*

As you release Uru from his misperceived role, it leaves an imprint in the blueprint of humans. Thus, it will become easier for all those who come after you to let go of their fear of Uru as well.

Uru will continue to be with you and the humans, because it is in his nature to observe separation and find ever-smoother and simpler ways to go beyond it.

*

Even if you change your assessment of Uru at a higher level of your consciousness, do not expect it to change your reactions at the micro level. Those are part of stimulus-response schemes that have dominated your being for a very, very long time. So *be patient* and have compassion for yourself when the micro level takes over once again.

Since you have chosen to become a conscious visitor in the dream of separation, waking up and deconditioning at the micro level must take place *slowly*. Therefore, we will go into the light body exercise presented in the last volume again in detail and let our new realizations flow in.

I am Aouwa, an Elder of Uru.

11. The Spectrum of Consciousness

I am Althar, the Crystal Dragon!

I have already talked about the importance of cultivating your awareness. Let me emphasize once again that it is the dedicated practice of this non-practice that will gently and surely liberate you from everything that sustains your belief in separation.

As an extension of this practice, I suggested cultivating the light body, also called the "light body exercise." In this chapter and in the next, I will go into it in more detail. A better understanding of how and why this exercise works might encourage you to actually *do* it.

Before we begin the discourse, please review the chapter "The Magic of your Light Body" as presented in *"Althar – The Final Letting Go"* for preparation. Since this chapter is already very compressed, it would not be helpful to give an even more compact summary at this point.

*

Like the chapter you have just read, this chapter also has many levels of understanding that will only gradually unfold. So, please read this and the subsequent chapter very slowly and repeat it over the next days, weeks, and months. If you also *apply* what you read, you will certainly become aware of an ever-greater insight, which I transmit beyond words. You will finally *experience* it as true wisdom!

Let's begin by talking about the term "bliss." With bliss I describe the fusion of *all pleasant feelings.* They are all contained in their highest possible intensity, their essence, in bliss. When one is completely absorbed in pure consciousness, the feeling of bliss is the normal state.

Think of feelings that you, as a human, really relish. Say, beauty, love, peace, serenity, fulfillment, freedom, joy, to name a few. Imagine this multitude of feelings *melding into a single feeling.* This is similar to white light, which contains all colors. I denote the resulting composition of feelings as bliss.

We have said that ultimately there is only one reason why a person sets out to live through the next segment of his thread of time: *He wants to feel certain feelings.* Many of them *as* he progresses, and some he hopes to experience in the future, for example when a larger project is completed.

Since the typical human is subject to the false assumption that only the *exterior* can stimulate the desired feelings, he makes every possible effort to bring about the necessary *external* circumstances. Yet, whatever feeling he desires *is most certainly contained in bliss,* the feeling equivalent of your natural state. Therefore, it could be accessed *from within at any time,* without the need for external favorable circumstances.

*

There exists a very important connection between the feeling of bliss and the density of consciousness. Metaphorically it can be said that a densification of consciousness is identical with a lowering of its frequency. This has a serious effect:

By lowering the frequency of consciousness, part of the natural bliss of pure consciousness is veiled. The lower the frequency, the stronger the veiling.

The veiled feelings are not eliminated in any form, but an *inability to be naturally aware of them* arises in the slowly vibrating consciousness.

This has significant implications for all entities that exist in separation. For when a true self wants to experience a certain realm of separation from within, it needs a body that has the same density as the realm into which it enters. Thus in this body, depending on its density, *parts of the natural bliss are veiled.*

This creates a very powerful dynamic: Pure consciousness was *not aware* of the individual components of its bliss, but with the increased density of consciousness and the resulting veiling, *the entity that entered density now senses a lack!*

As a result, this entity *longs* for what it lacks! It wants to *get it back*, even if it cannot define exactly *what* it is missing. For before it entered into this density, it was *not even aware* of the existence of the now veiled parts of bliss!

So, what does the entity do? It tries to *compensate* for this lack with a *substitute*. It tries to find something *on the outside* that can relieve this lack felt on the inside. This substitute then becomes the object of desire, and the entity tries to *create circumstances* in order to obtain the substitute.

However, if it succeeds in doing so and this lack is relieved, the *veiling is not removed*. Rather, the sensation of relief is like a *reminder* of the essence of the feeling, which is veiled in the density.

Since polarity is inherently impermanent, *no substitute can bring about lasting relief from the feeling of lack.* Instead, any substitute sooner or later becomes a source of frustration.

*

Now, please take some time to feel into the essence of each of the following feelings: safety, love, clarity, bliss.

*

Safety, love, clarity, and bliss correspond to the four major levels of the human existence, ranging from the slowest vibration of physical existence to the highest non-vibration of pure consciousness. We could certainly address more than just four levels, but they are sufficient for our discussion.

Other feelings mentioned in the light body exercise, such as completion and freedom, also play an important role, but are not as connected to the physical and non-physical form as are safety, love, clarity, and bliss. We will now take a deeper look at these feelings and their connection to the density of consciousness.

The first major level below pure consciousness is the level of the mind. It corresponds to the *mental body* of the human being. The mind is not yet physical, although one could say that each thought also has a form. At this level, the feeling of *clarity* is veiled due to the density.

Pure consciousness is in a state of "I know that I know," but with the lowering of consciousness to the level of the mind, questions and doubts suddenly arise. The thinking human recognizes with a shudder: "I know that I *don't* know!" Therefore, *he tries to understand his thoughts by means of thoughts*. He lacks *clarity* and wants to restore it through the detour of comprehension.

But no matter how hard he tries, he simply can't achieve absolute clarity in polarity! Take a look at human scientists. They earn their living by researching what they don't yet understand. And how many times in the past have they revised what they thought was right and *clear?* The mind keeps asking for more details. Any mental understanding thus immediately raises new questions and is, if at all, only a fleeting and fragile substitute for true clarity.

Additionally, the mind has also reached the borders of the recognizable. Physicists have had to learn that they cannot measure anything smaller than a certain size or that lasts less than a certain time interval. These limits are produced by physics itself and are not due to inadequate measurement techniques. Although these limits may be very small, they act as *impenetrable walls* that prevent a clear understanding of the physical. Whatever is going on behind these walls *will remain a mystery!* A mystery may have its own beauty, but it certainly lacks clarity – *it is incomprehensible!*

Since mental understanding is not so suitable as a substitute for clarity, the entities on this level of density therefore strive for *control*. They try to create an environment in which *everything goes according to plan.* As a result, they are *reasonably clear* about what's usually going to happen next in their controlled environment. They use control as substitute to alleviate the lack of clarity.

This goes so far that even an entity brave enough to allow change does everything it possibly can to *control* the effects of change. I think you know what I mean.

*

At the next level, we come to the emotions and the emotional body of the human. Emotions arise only in an entity which inhabits a sufficiently dense body and is additionally identified with a set of beliefs forming its false identities. The density of this level veils what humans call *love*.

Love has become a very ambiguous term. Here, we use love as a synonym for unconditional acceptance. However, *love and identification cannot co-exist within an entity!*

Identification involves a demarcation and thus a separation from the other. But as long as there is a border between two beings, *love is impossible!* So, the entities learn very quickly that love is something extremely rare, and that they have to make do with a substitute. Thus, rather than hoping in vain for love, they instead crave *conditional acceptance* by the other.

Almost all emotions have a direct relation to the feeling of love, or to the sensation of lack of love. Therefore, a high percentage of a person's activities can be seen as an attempt to compensate for the lack of love. The emotions act as a compass that is based on experiences and beliefs to find conditional acceptance and avoid rejection.

Of course, *moments* of true love *can* occur between two beings when both take off their armor and experience a kind of fusion. But since the experience of love is so overwhelming that it threatens to annihilate the beings, they quickly put their armor on again. What remains after such an intense moment of love is a well-kept memory of this fusion, combined with the *hope of repeating the experience in the future.*

You may have heard stories of two humans, who after sharing a moment of love, clung to each other even though it turned out they were not exactly compatible in daily life. Sometimes it is said that stories like this *can even be spread over several lifetimes!* I can tell you, love, and especially the lack of it, are the driving forces behind most occurrences – and the subject of far too many lyrics.

In fact, *any beings* can share moments of love with each other. Love is not a question of gender, age, appearance, or hormones. But instead of being open and available to experience love with any entity at any moment, it is a widespread belief that love is reserved for a *single* partner or a *small selected number* of close family members.

Beings at this level lack lasting love, but there is no way to realize it as long as they hold on to their identities. Whenever they experience love, it is but for a short period of time. And no matter how hard they try to create a lasting feeling of love, they will inevitably fail because *their identities will not allow it!* Thus, they settle for conditional acceptance of their false identities through other false identities.

Sounds disappointing, doesn't it? The good news is, of course, that actually *no other entity* is needed to feel love. In fact, it doesn't even make a difference! Although the sex might be better. But what is sex compared to a never-ending cosmic orgasm! Oops, I guess I digress. Or not.

*

Finally, at the physical level, the vulnerability of the human body comes into play. The greatest additional lack caused by the veiling at this level is the *lack of safety*. The body *can die at any mo-ment*, and no matter what a person does to prolong his life, his body will eventually perish.

To compensate for the lack of safety, humans do everything possible to protect their bodies. They seek refuge in fortresses, be they of stones, beliefs, or knowledge. They protect their bodies with muscles, weapons, and fighting techniques. They hoard money and goods to be prepared for the worst. They join forces with others to organize guards, police forces, and armies. They invest a large part of their finances in health care.

However, it is completely obvious to everyone that *no substitute whatsoever* can even begin to compensate for the lack of safety at the level of the body. Thus, the typical human goes into *denial and seeks distraction.*

The physical body is *the* symbol of separation par excellence and has the lowest vibration of consciousness. Down here, the dream world feels *so real.* Down here, the fear of death, the fear of letting go of one's identity, the fear of being extinguished from existence, the fear of encountering Uru, is *so overwhelming and omnipresent*, that a true substitute for the lack of safety is not even at hand.

*

A lack of bliss, clarity, and love is a burden, but you can survive it.

But a lack of safety in a physical body is brutal, *because you know you can't survive it!*

That's why hypnosis was necessary!

You had to be made to want to stay physical – *at all costs!*

Because the hope was precisely that you would overcome *separation itself,* and not just rescue yourself from the physical realm to a more comfortable, less dense realm. *That's where you came from,* so nothing would have been achieved!

*

Isn't it amazing how simple and clear things are? As the density of consciousness increases, more and more parts of its natural bliss become *veiled.* When an entity enters a denser realm of existence, it perceives the veiling as *lack.* So it tries to compensate for this lack by searching for a *substitute* on the outside. But since nothing can persist in polarity, any compensation by a substitute is at best *temporary* and often becomes a new source of frustration. Hence, this lack has to be compensated for *again and again.* And typically, an *ever-higher dose* is needed! Thus, this being acts out the mantra of separation: Enough is not enough!

In a way, the craziest thing about it is that a human, despite its aversion to dying, can only appreciate life at all precisely *because of* the knowledge of his own impending death! Just imagine for a second what it would mean for you, if you had to continue your present life for all eternity. I mean, not just a few hundred years on top – *I mean forever!*

*

The light body exercise is designed to compensate for the perceived lack along the spectrum of consciousness – *without* using fleeting external objects and circumstances.

Through this exercise, you will become more and more familiar with your true nature. You will slowly let go of all attempts to compensate for lack through activities on the outside. Eventually, you will release the existential fear of extinction that arises as you release your bindings to the physical body. Over time, your physical body will relax more and more, and mimic the light body with more success.

By the way, humans are the only beings in all of existence that can experience the whole spectrum of consciousness, from the bliss of pure consciousness to the lack of safety as a body. This is precisely why the path to enlightenment is lead through the incarnation as a human on Earth.

After this verbose prologue, it's time to get practical and turn once more to the light body exercise. See you tomorrow!

I am Althar, a being of crystalline bliss.

12. The Light Body Exercise

I am Althar, the Crystal Dragon!

Before we get started, I'd like to make a note on terminology. Instead of using the term "light body exercise," I'd much rather speak of "cultivating your light body." This term is nobler and much more appropriate, because it is by no means an ordinary human exercise in the sense of a gymnastic or relaxation exercise. But because "cultivating your light body" is too bulky to use consistently, I will bow to the human language and use the term light body exercise.

Why is an exercise necessary at all? Because unfortunately, it is simply not enough just to accept true wisdom or marvel at it with a gaping mouth. Rather, it must be *experienced*. Only when it is confirmed from within by your own experience can it unfold its full liberating power.

But here lies the problem. *Humans tend to go to the extreme.* They become all too easily fanatical, dogmatic, or lethargic, but all too rarely *pragmatic*. Fanaticism and dogmatism correspond to "doing," lethargy to "doing nothing at all." Both are not exactly beneficial on the path of enlightenment, because in one case new patterns are created and consolidated, while in the other, existing patterns are not dissolved. So, is it any wonder that there have been so few enlightened humans thus far?

But fortunately, we are pragmatic through and through, because with the light body exercise, we are *doing the non-doing!* And we do it *passionately and with devotion* – at least it is my wish that my messages will have this effect.

The light body exercise is a *non-doing,* for ultimately it is only about becoming aware of one's own true nature. *What could be more natural?* If one wanted to achieve this through *doing*, it is as if water wanted to get wet through doing.

It is also a non-doing because it takes place *only in the present moment.* Although there will be a lot of positive results in the course of linear time, these also unfold *in a natural way!* Neither are results the goal, nor does time play a role. The integration with the light body happens *moment by moment* and will finally release you from your body and from time! Just like that.

The light body exercise, however, is a *doing* in the sense that you must *create the leeway* for yourself to *actually perform it!*

You don't have time for this? No problem. Put the book down and come back in a few years. But first a few hints: It certainly won't get any easier when you are older, your body hurts and you have accumulated more patterns. Also, one hour of light body exercise replaces two hours of sleep. So, if you still have time to sleep, there shouldn't be any problems with the leeway you need. All you have to do is choose between sleeping and awakening. *Do it now!*

*

Still here? Great! Or have a few years passed in the meantime? Also great! In any case, it starts now.

During the light body exercise, you *intensify* your awareness of the feelings that the human consciousness is no longer naturally aware of due to the veiling. It is important to understand that it is *not you*, as a human being, who *creates* the feelings. Rather, they are already present as components of the bliss of your light body! It is only a matter of *becoming aware of them!* This has many beneficial effects.

On the surface, the awareness of the feelings *compensates for the lack* felt on the human level. This makes it more and more unnecessary for you to strive for compensation on the outside. By acting out your patterns less and less, they will eventually dissolve. I call this *deconditioning*.

Through the intensification of awareness, a *desensitizing* occurs. This is essential for embodied ascension, because the untrained human usually finds the intensity of the pure consciousness' bliss *overwhelming*. As a result, he either shies back or the bliss feels so *irresistible* to him that he enters into it, never to come back. There is nothing wrong with the latter, but with respect to embodiment, the game would be over. Therefore, a desensitizing is urgently recommended.

As you become aware of and intensify various pleasant feelings *simultaneously*, you gradually become accustomed to the intensity of the bliss of your unveiled natural state. Figuratively, the combination of feelings corresponds to the union of different colored lights into unbroken white light.

As a side effect of intensification and ever-more penetrating clarity, *everything hidden within you will come to the surface,* be it fears, guilt, shame, trauma, or suppressed desires. Since nothing can withstand pure consciousness, all this ballast will simply dissolve *through the use of your inner power! Just like that!* And it has to, because there is no way to approach the final letting go as long as you drag something with you! Even the smallest piece of luggage binds you like a heavy anchor to the world of separation.

In addition to the effects of desensitizing and deconditioning, your physical body, by its very nature, mimics the light body that is within and all around it, and thereby gets increasingly integrated into it.

*

To simplify the intensification, it is helpful to imagine a special dimmer during the light body exercise. With this dimmer, you regulate the intensity with which *you allow yourself to perceive a certain feeling.*

The special thing about the dimmer is that it does not regulate the intensity in small increments, like that of a lamp. Instead, by turning the dimmer you can *multiply* the perceived intensity by any amount. So, it works *exponentially* and allows you to cover *the entire intensity spectrum.*

For example, with such a dimmer you could increase the intensity of the room temperature to the temperature inside the sun by turning it a few notches. Inside the sun, there are several million degrees, so if the dimmer would work just linearly, you would have to turn it until exhaustion.

Incidentally, the comparison with the temperature spectrum is very well transferable to the intensity spectrum of feelings. Let's take clarity as an example. In fact, it's not about raising your awareness of clarity from 25 to 30 degrees Clarity, *but to 30 million degrees Clarity!* Because this high temperature corresponds roughly to the intensity of the *essence* of clarity. Why else would the compression have to be so extremely strong? Because of 5 degrees more or less?

Remember how we stepped into the sun in one of the first messages. At that time, however, there was one remarkable difference: we entered the sun *as consciousness* while your body remained on Earth. Now it is more like *we are moving the sun towards your body,* so we have to go step by step – even if they are big steps.

The multiplier you assign to your dimmer is entirely up to you. It could be a two. Turning the dimmer one notch would double the intensity. Turn it three notches, and the intensity will increase eightfold. If you use a multiplier of 10, then turning the dimmer three notches will increase the intensity a thousand times. In fact, the dimmer is quite a cool gadget.

You may remember that when I presented the light body exercise in the previous volume, I emphasized that you should proceed *cautiously* and *not push* anything. *That is still true!* But – just between you and me – now and then it's fun to put the pedal to the metal, isn't it? Not that I, as a dragon, would ever have to rush or push anything, but I have heard of *mature* adepts who were able to deal with huge increases... But it's still up to you to choose the right measure! So let's just translate "cautious" into "start with a multiplier of two."

The reason why I am introducing the concept of exponential intensification at all is the following: If you were to increase the intensity very slowly, you would only increase your comfort zone a little. This is quite appropriate until you can assess the reactions of your physical body. But once you realize you can go *far* beyond the usual and then actually *do it,* you will experience a very important effect:

Your doubt vanishes!

It simply puffs away!

And with it, any notion of lack goes out the window. The term "lack" itself becomes completely meaningless! When you experience this effect for the first time, you will *know from within* that you are not just playing a mental game with yourself. Instead, you will marvel at your true nature and know:

This is the direct way to the final letting go!

*

In addition to intensifying the awareness of feelings, I would like to introduce another component. In a previous message, I spoke about the name of a true self. In fact, the name of a true self cannot really be spoken or phonetically represented. Rather, it is like a multidimensional light pattern associated with a polyphonic humming. It is a fusion of bliss and the distilled wisdom of all the experiences the true self has ever had.

In a way, bliss is universal – it is the same for every entity in separation. But the fusion of bliss with the wisdom attained by a true self while traversing the Second Round of Creation *makes this true self unique!* This is his *signature* by which he is recognized by other true selves.

Of course, your true self, dear reader, also has such a signature. *But even that was veiled by the compression and hypnosis*, so that you completely forgot your origin.

Therefore, the final step of the light body exercise is to allow yourself to become aware of the deeply personal signature of your true self. The associated indescribable feeling will give you the certainty of being "at home." But there is more to it than that:

Through your awareness of the signature of your true self, the hypnosis that took place on the micro level of your consciousness is reversed!

Uru has made sure that *only you* can reverse the hypnosis. And the *key*, dear friend, *is the signature of your true self.*

Again, use the dimmer to control the intensity with which you want to be aware of your signature. However, in this case it is *very important to proceed gently and cautiously! There is no need to hurry!*

When your signature, which is vibrating in the light body, touches the hypnotized part of your consciousness that is bound to the physical, it is awakened from hypnosis. This awakened consciousness will then immediately recognize the light body as its true home and *connect with it also!*

This is *the* essential building block in the integration of the light body and the physical body. The formerly hypnotized part of consciousness now becomes the link between the light body and the physical body.

The integration is a *process!* It will *gradually* unfold in your linear time without you having to control any aspect of it! Lean back, enjoy – *and stay out!*

Let me repeat the following fundamental point one more time: You *do nothing* to create or amplify a feeling. The feeling is already present in your light body! When you turn the dimmer, you simply allow yourself to become more and more aware of one facet of your innate bliss, and finally of your signature.

In other words:

You just surrender to your true nature!

Thus, the veiling is overcome and the dream of separation goes where all dreams go after waking up.

*

Now we will go through the light body exercise step by step.

At the beginning of each exercise, first become aware of *what* you are about to do. *You will open up to your Godself and fuse with it more and more!* Could there be something more sublime? Could there be something more important? Therefore, adopt an inner attitude of dignity that corresponds to this intention.

Then, choose a *stable* posture, because you will let go of the conscious control over your body. The easiest way is to lie down or sit down. If you choose to sit down, *take a royal stance!* Sit upright and stretch your spine. This not only has a direct impact on your emotional body, but also allows your abdomen to move freely while your breathing finds its natural rhythm.

When you have collected yourself, become aware of your true self. *From the level of your true self,* hold the intent to have a light body – and it will be there. Become aware that it surrounds and permeates your whole physical body, emotional body, and mental body. It is therefore much larger than your physical body. Actually, it is completely boundless.

*

Now, become aware of the feeling of *safety*. It is part of the bliss of your light body and available to you. To that end, it can be helpful if you first remember a situation in which you felt very unsafe, for example when you were flying through strong turbulence in an airplane. In this way, you can feel the *relative* safety you are in right now.

As soon as you can clearly be aware of safety, let go of the memory and use your dimmer to *multiply the intensity of your awareness!* Allow yourself to surrender more and more to the safety of your light body! Enjoy it! Feel safety *around* you, feel it *inside* you, feel it in every *cell* and every *atom*. Feel it throughout the light body *that you are!* Nothing can harm your light body, *because nothing else has reality!* Thus, you are *safe!* Use your dimmer wisely to become aware of an ever-greater intensity of safety!

It is important that you do not allow yourself to be distracted by body reactions throughout the exercise! Tears may come to you, your body may tremble, surges of emotion may flood you – *just let it all happen and observe it!*

It is also very important not to be *carried away* by the enthusiasm that may arise within as soon as you feel the enormous effects produced by turning the dimmer. At first, you will most likely not be able to resist this, but with a little practice in observing, you will realize that these are false identities that suddenly feel your "power" and want to seize it greedily. Even the good old saber-toothed tiger could be brought back to life and burst with energy. Observe it and let it go – no matter how seductive it may seem!

*

Next, become aware of the feeling of *love* that is present in your light body. Again, it may be helpful if you first recall a memory of a moment of love. It could be love you have experienced with a person, perhaps even with your very first romantic love, or with a pet, or nature. As soon as you are aware of the feeling of love, let go of the memory and stay with the pure feeling.

Then, use your dimmer to increase your aware-ness of love! The light body then appears more and more like *the essence of love itself.* And this love is *for you!* It is *absolutely unconditional!* Nothing you don't like about yourself plays a role for it, because this love *knows about the unreality of your dream!*

Feel that there is *nothing outside of you that could convey a deeper love!* Feel your false iden-tities simply dissolve as you realize that *they have lost all function!* You are in complete love with yourself. There is simply no longer any need to beg for conditional acceptance through false iden-tities on the outside. You are a vessel of love, overflowing with love. Thus, your emotional body comes more and more to rest *until it finally dissolves completely.* Then, you will be so free that *you can no longer be called a limited human.*

*

Next, become aware of the *clarity* of your light body. The light body does not have a single question, for it *knows that it knows!* Use your dimmer to increase your awareness of this crystal-clear clarity! Feel how it *relaxes your mental body.* The mental body can release all its desperate efforts to control and analyze. It realizes: "Things *are* simple if I simply let them be."

Now, simultaneously become aware of the safety, love, and clarity that are in you and all around you. *Fuse them!* Then use the dimmer to intensify the awareness of this fused feeling!

Bliss is the fusion of all feelings that a human finds pleasant. For an untrained person, safety, love, and clarity are already overwhelming, but you have chosen *to go far beyond that.*

Therefore, add more wonderful feelings. First, I recommend my personal favorite: beauty. Then completeness, freedom, contentedness, joy, and whatever else may come to mind. Fuse all this into a *single* awareness and use the dimmer to multiply its intensity. In this way, *you approach more and more the bliss of your true nature.*

Know that at this point, *Ila* will be very palpable for you. She is the *Goddess of Bliss* and also the *Unborn Goddess of Feminine Beingness*. Perhaps you will feel her birthing nature, her ability to bring forth *true creation.*

Maybe you will also become aware of the part of *yourself* that, like Ila, never entered separation. From a human perspective, this part feels like the essence of the feminine. In a way, both you and your true self have forgotten this part – *but it has not forgotten you!* While you remain in this highest possible awareness, Ila helps you to *remember all that you have always been.*

I remind you once again – you should not interfere with the reactions of your body. Relax all your muscles. Let the breath come and go without controlling it. Just let the surges of old and ancient memories, together with the accompanying body reactions, happen. The physical body *mimics* what is all around it and thereby releases all kinds of tension and repressed feelings. *This is its natural behavior.* Let go of the desire to control it.

*

Finally, become aware of the signature of your true self. Its multidimensional hum and light are everywhere in and around your physical body, melded with the feeling of bliss.

By the way, the awareness of your *signature* is very closely connected with the awareness of your *inner power,* for both are expressions of your unlimited sovereignty!

Allow your signature to enter deeply, deeply, deeply into your cell structure, down to the level of subatomic particles. Select a cell of your body and visualize an atom of the DNA of that cell.

Become aware of how your signature simultaneously embraces and penetrates the atom. Feel how the whole atom is gently brought into resonance with your signature and how this resonance is *slowly transmitted to all atoms of your body.*

Do nothing actively at this level! Just be aware of your signature and watch passively what is happening at the micro level.

You might feel the subconscious fear of your hypnotized consciousness meeting Uru. For the first time, you might feel the guilt and shame of being physical. You could perceive the survival impulses of your cells. Animal drives and sexual cravings could rise in you. *Observe all this!* You *know* that you are safe! You *know* who you are! You *know* that you lack nothing. *You are only observing the remnants of old dreams!*

Use the dimmer to increase your awareness of your signature. This will awaken the hypnotized consciousness bound to the atomic level. As already mentioned, apply the dimmer here with *special care*, because:

Your signature is the key to freeing you from the physical!

It should be a great relief to know that you have this key, and that you can *turn it completely at any time,* in case you think it is appropriate – if you know what I mean.

*

How you end the light body exercise is entirely at your discretion. But try to be *as aware as possible* when you begin to move your body. You will then be able to observe how your expanded awareness returns to the limited human mode – *and there's nothing wrong with that!*

If you do this exercise over and over again, you will notice enormous changes. Not only in your physical body, but also in your emotional and mental body. You will gradually correct all distortions of your perceptions and thus, see reality more and more *as it really is!*

At some point, you will perform the entire light body exercise *in a single moment!* When you realize that you are dreaming, you *instantly shift into your light body and its bliss.* Your light body will then perceive existence with the *Eye of Suchness.*

Through persistent practice, you will eventually realize that you are *no longer returning to the human limitations.* You are now continuously in full awareness of your true nature and your light body. In other words:

The final letting go has occurred in a natural way!

You have freed yourself from the grip of separation and can still visit the dream worlds of separation with your light body.

Thus, you have realized embodied ascension.

*

I would like to add some comments regarding the physical level. No matter, dear reader, how you deceive yourself, no matter how enlightened or cool you think you are – *letting go of the bindings to the physical body is the most difficult step a human can ever take!*

Why? Because at the level of the body, everything seems to be *so real,* and here, your physical existence is confronted with its fear of death. Moreover, it is not a death like any other, as *it will be your final death!* You will *never again* experience the world of separation through a body as you have been used to for ages.

Are you really ready for that?

At the higher levels, embodied ascension could be seen as a kind of game. What do you have to lose if you play on those levels? You're bored anyway, so why not experiment with some new beliefs and approaches to life? But when it comes to the physical level, it becomes existential – *because here, not only your present life, but also your physical future in its entirety is threatened!*

Therefore, if your physical body should signal "Enough!" during the light body exercise, *reduce the intensity!* Continue to observe what is going on without judging or regretting. See with the Eye of Suchness so that the perceived is exposed to your pure consciousness. If your body signals approval after a pause, then continue the exercise. If not, end it or just stay with cultivating your awareness.

The awakening from the *dream of being a body has to happen gradually,* otherwise you would just leave your body for good. But "gradually" implies a certain potential for frustration, as you probably have expectations of results despite all good intentions. So, you will have to be compassionate with yourself again and again, because so often you will notice that you have lost yourself once more in the dream of separation.

Ultimately, however, it is always a matter of a moment – for a moment of pure awareness is a moment of enlightenment. And so is a moment of bliss on all levels of your existence *a moment of embodied ascension.*

Go forth, dear reader, go forth! Now is not the time to hesitate or give up. You are close. *Patiently surrender yourself to yourself again and again.*

This is how the Opus Magnum is realized.

I am Althar, a most blissful light body.

13. Opus Magnum

I am Aouwa, a true self in expression!

Now I will convey a message that will shake the very foundations of your being. It will defy your notions of common sense and undermine your potential scientific education. It will challenge the humility behind which you love to hide, and it will certainly cause anxiety. For if what I am about to tell you is actually true, then *you* would be the one who is fully responsible for *everything* that seems to happen. Yes, I mean for *everything*!

The *realization* of what I am about to convey is called the *Opus Magnum, the Great Work*. In many of the preceding messages in this book series, Althar and I have already alluded to it in order to lay the groundwork. But now that you are approaching the final letting go, it is time for you to *accept and realize what follows from letting go of the belief in separation.*

If you are not yet ready to accept the consequences of letting go of separation, be assured that this message will still find its place in your consciousness. It will slowly mature in you and reveal more and more of its truth. Sooner or later, be it in this life or another, you will be back at this point and retest yourself.

The message as such is very brief, yet very profound. In the following chapter, Althar will develop it further and place it into a larger context.

To convey the message, we need an appropriate stage. That is why I invite you to travel to a place that is ideal for it: the sun. You were already there with Althar, remember? So, leave your body where it is and go into the sun.

*

Take a look at Earth from the perspective of the sun. Isn't she beautiful? Sure, from the viewpoint of a physical body, Earth can be very rough. But seen from the sun, Earth is an incomparable gem in the universe.

Now imagine holding Earth in your arms like you would hold a baby.

*

Holding a baby in your arms is already a very special experience. *But holding the whole Earth is...* not to be described with words. It awakens all the love you have for this special place.

Although you have had many difficult experiences on Earth, you have also had wonderful insights, breakthroughs and encounters there.

Above all, you know one thing: Earth is *the* place! This is the one place in the universe where the belief in separation can finally be let go, so that the Second Round of Creation can come to an end.

Now, after all the preparation we have been through, I ask you this:

If there is no separation, where does the inside end? Where does the outside begin?

*

So many humans dream of enlightenment, but in reality, they only hope for a more pleasant life, less frustration, and a few magic tricks to fulfill their wishes. Or they just yearn for some new spiritual details for their perpetual search.

But even the truly sincere shy away from accepting the obvious. Thus, they remain in separation.

Are you brave enough to face the simplest and most significant of all questions?

Then, I ask you again:

If there is no separation, where does the inside end? Where does the outside begin?

*

Are you ready to accept the truth?

Are you ready to take full responsibility?

Are you ready to embrace all that you are?

Then, dear friend, let me state the obvious:

You are your own universe!

And by universe, I do not just mean the physical universe. I mean All-That-Is!

*

In *your universe*, you are the *only* ruler. There is neither inside nor outside! You have no center! Whatever appears to be outside of you and comes to you as perception is actually *you!*

You are the mirror cabinet, all mirrors, and all mirrored intentions as well as the initiator, receiver, and interpreter of all perceptions.

The physical universe you experience right now *is you!*

You are the mountains, the oceans, and the wind. You are the plants, the animals, and all of the humans. You are the stars and the galaxies. You are time, space, and energy.

If you see with the Eye of Separation, you establish and solidify borders. You make distinctions between you and not-you; between the perceiver and perceived. Thus, I say: You are not what you perceive.

By fully accepting your true heritage and seeing with the Eye of Suchness, separation ceases. Now you see things as they truly are and you recognize:

The things you see are truly you!

Thus, I say: *You are your own universe.*

*

Once you fully accept and realize the obvious that results from letting go of separation, you are birthing yourself into the Third Round of Creation.

Then you realize that you are an *extension of the one I Am.* You are sovereign and simultaneously one with All-That-Is.

Thus, the Opus Magnum is realized.

I am Aouwa.

14. The Big Picture

I am Althar, the Crystal Dragon!

To human consciousness clinging to limitations and identity, the Opus Magnum seems like the delusion of a megalomaniac brain shaken by fantasies of omnipotence. But as I have said so many times, consciousness is extraordinarily wondrous. So wondrous that it can dream of a tiny bubble which then actually has the arrogance to regard itself as *separate* from the whole. Thus, the question arises whether insisting on separation is not the actual fantasy of omnipotence, and whether the realization of the Opus Magnum equates the return to the normal state. Well, I guess I've made my answer to that question clear by now. But, of course, I acknowledge to the limited human consciousness its skepticism – at least I make every effort to appear to do so. To that end, it benefits me greatly that I exist beyond time and therefore, know frustration only from hearsay.

In order to maintain the semblance of, and if necessary, alleviate your skepticism a little, dear reader, I will now try to summarize the essential stages of exploring separation in all brevity. This might allow you to see the Opus Magnum more as a natural unfolding and less as megalomania. Then, we will enter the greatest mystery of all and dare to place the Opus Magnum in an even greater context.

As so often mentioned before, I would like to stress once again that the metaphors I have chosen are meant *as aids* for a human to see its experiences in a broader context. It is still about freeing oneself from the illusion of separation with *appropriate illusions.* Therefore, dear reader, do not become entangled in questions of detail and doubts. In general, if doubt arises, choose the Eye of Suchness – *and every question and every answer shall lose its relevance!*

So here is first a summary of existence in separation, also known as the Second Round of Creation.

*

True selves suddenly find themselves in the Second Round of Creation. Why? This is a mystery about which could only be speculated.

In the Second Round of Creation, the true selves are subject to the belief that there is separation. At first, they are *not aware* of this belief. They *experience* what it means to exist in separation. Therefore, they feel isolated from the beginning and long for completion.

A true self is consciousness. It has the ability to be aware of itself and to have intents. How and why it produces intentions is a mystery that can be called creativity.

Since a true self in the Second Round of Creation holds on to the belief in separation, all its intentions also contain the element of separation.

Pure energy is a "crystallized" form of the true self that reflects intents. So, pure energy is still the true self. It has nothing to do with what humans experience as physical energies.

Separation brings forth ever-more separation. In a sense, all potential expressions stemming from separation spring into existence simultaneously. I call this an ocean of oceans of scene spheres. They need no explicit representation, but they exist as implicit potentials *within the true self.*

The scene spheres cover the entire spectrum of densities that separation can produce. A true self is at the lowest density level. It can emit any number of portions of itself to explore separation. Thus, different parts of a true self can meet as different life forms, or as different incarnations beyond linear time.

Every scene sphere can be experienced from within. The conscious portion of the true self that dives into a scene sphere uses its own pure energy to reflect the conditions within the scene sphere upon itself. Since this part of the consciousness does not perceive the actual process of reflection, his experiences seem to be induced from the "outside."

While this part of consciousness penetrates into ever greater densities, at some point it believes that it *is* a certain form. First, it identifies with an ethereal body and finally, with a physical body that seems to be bound to a place in space.

The constant progression from scene sphere to scene sphere creates the illusion of linear time.

If a being enters a scene sphere in which different entities appear, it has a common experience with these beings. However, each of these entities applies its own interpretations, and thus experiences its own version of the scene. All beings within separation live exclusively in their personal reality.

Identification with a physical body gives the impression that everything experienced is extraordinarily *real*. The body exists in time and space, and the changes in the environment from scene to scene seem to be caused by energies coming from outside the body. *Yet, everything is still happening in the true self and its pure energy!*

By crossing the scene spheres, the entity develops an ever-deeper understanding of what it has experienced, as well as wisdom. Therefore, at some point, the entity recognizes separation for what it is: a belief. Furthermore, the constant repetitions caused by separation become more and more obvious, and are finally perceived as a threatening standstill.

The standstill is also a synonym for the fact that there is no true creation within separation. Sooner or later, this realization comes to every entity, no matter in which density of consciousness it exists.

Therefore, at some point every being is faced with the question of *how to get out of separation.*

Each true self and each of its emanations are at all times free to let go of the belief in separation. However, an entity that exists in separation equates letting go of separation with the extinction of its own existence. In addition, separation has the quality of appearing more and more real the more one gets involved with it. Thus, blueprints, patterns, traumas, unfulfilled desires, fear, guilt, and shame lead to a constant reaffirmation of the belief that separation is real, and is the only way to exist.

Attempts to overcome separation were carried out at various densities without lasting success. A human, however, who encompasses the entire spectrum of consciousness, may eventually allow the belief in separation to be released *once and for all*.

The keys to freeing yourself from separation are true wisdom, cultivating awareness, and compassion for oneself.

When the letting go of separation occurs, it leads to *enlightenment* – the natural state of pure consciousness. With enlightenment of the human, the letting go of separation permeates throughout all of the human's true self. Thus, the true self *ascends* and finds itself beyond separation in its natural state. It is enriched by all the experiences and wisdom it has gained during its experience of the Second Round of Creation.

With ascension, the pure energy of the true self loses its inherent character of separation. The primary forces of polarity, fire and water, are integrated and transmuted into *liquid light*. Liquid light is also called *new energy*.

Now the ascended true self naturally brings forth true creation – a creation that is not distorted by separation. Thus, the standstill is overcome and the true self has entered the Third Round of Creation.

The ascended true self recognizes that it is both sovereign and non-separated from other true selves. This resembles a hologram of true selves.

As separation never was real in the first place, even the true selves who found themselves in the void were already part of that very hologram! But the belief in separation veiled their knowingness. Thus, you could say there was exactly *one* pondering of separation and *one* dream of separation shared by the hologram of all true selves.

*

An enlightened human can choose to remain present in the shared dream of physical reality. To facilitate this, he can try to integrate his physical body into his light body.

The light body is a conscious projection from the plane of the true self into the dream of separation. It is free of limitations. Ideally, the light body was already cultivated when the human approached the final letting go. Staying in physical reality is also possible without the light body, but empirically, it is not long in duration.

A "human" who remains on Earth while being in a state of *permanent* enlightenment has realized embodied ascension. This entity may seem like a human, but can no longer be called a human.

That was the short version. We get the shortest short version by omitting the details:

You are experiencing a shared and rather seductive dream of separation. Let go of the belief in separation by cultivating your awareness and the dream will cease. Oh, no one can do that for you.

*

The following question might come up: How many true selves are there?

Well, what we have laid out above actually does not even require *two* true selves, does it? Any "other" true self could have been made up simply by the belief in separation, just as you create all sorts of characters in your dreams at night.

But what if, dear reader, what if indeed *you* were the only true self?

What if there really was only you? Only you as pure consciousness?

Could you stand it?

Would you be overwhelmed by loneliness? In spite of all your creator abilities? In spite of all your bliss?

Imagine that for a while! How does that feel?

*

If you were the *only* true self and therefore the one pure consciousness, then perhaps you would want to produce equals with whom you could share your being. Equals to whom you give *everything* you are so that you can share your *whole* being. Maybe you would want to "separate" parts of yourself to create equals.

Maybe, just maybe, that's how it all started. Perhaps pure consciousness has pondered the impossible – *separation* – through which parts of itself became immersed in separation. Parts that here we call true selves, found themselves suddenly exposed to the impossibility of separation. True selves who traversed the strange worlds of separation, and thus became unique characters through their experiences.

Maybe this pondering of separation was accompanied by the knowingness that separation was not real. Maybe this knowingness made itself felt to the true selves through all sorts of intuition, hints, nudges, situations, sages, and even dragons. Perhaps this knowingness could also be called an *Ambassador of Creation.*

Then, when a true self finally emerged out of separation, it rediscovered its oneness with pure consciousness, even if pure consciousness was no longer what it once was.

So, the true selves would be brothers and sisters in the deepest sense of the word. They would be sovereign and yet connected. They could bring forth true creations and share their joy in them.

Since separation in itself is an *impossibility*, the thought of it had already disappeared with its emergence. In a mysterious way, though, nothing was the same afterwards as it was before.

*

Well, unfortunately, it remains a mystery how the true selves came into existence, right? So it would certainly be unwise to have a firm opinion on this subject. But approaching the mystery playfully is great fun – and who can say that one might not even touch the truth?

However, as soon as *you* fully emerge from separation you will be in the company of those who have already ascended. Not only will you be able to bring forth true creation, but you will know that you could bring forth equals without them having to go through the Second Round of Creation.

That's a great prospect, isn't it?

*

Initially, the big picture will be an intellectual concept that can lead to pronounced discomfort. But the more you get involved, the more sense it will make. The more sense it makes, the easier life will be.

You will begin to live simultaneously inside and outside the dream of separation. For some time, it will be like a flicker, back and forth. Then, in a quiet moment, you will notice that the flickering has stopped. You will stretch your consciousness, wipe a tear out of the Eye of Suchness, and accept your full creatorship.

What an unnatural idea – *separation* – yet, what a journey it provided!

Dear friend, all this has already happened. As you allow your dream of separation to dissolve, as you let go of all the attachments in your dream, as your dream becomes more and more joyful, we are already preparing your welcome party.

Does it matter how much longer it will take for you? I'll tell you a secret: Every true self that has ever ascended instantly realized that it didn't take *any time at all!* For time is a symptom of separation, and the *entire* Second Round of Creation took place the moment the thought of separation arose.

I am Althar, the celestial bartender, already preparing a gorgeous cocktail of fluid light with a hint of stardust for your welcome party.

15. The Transmission of the Light

I am Althar, the Crystal Dragon!

I feel honored and proud, dear reader, to have shared so many experiences with you. As you know, all the words were only carriers of a truth that is much more sublime and at the same time simpler than words could ever express. That is why it is said that the transmission of the light of true wisdom occurs from heart to heart, beyond words.

The moment you completely let go of separation and realize the Opus Magnum, you will recognize all the visible and invisible helpers you have encountered on your long journeys as a separated entity. These helpers came to you in many disguises to support you.

It could have been in the smile of a beggar, in the calm presence of a stranger, or while exchanging eye contact with a passer-by. It could have been a book, a guru, an angel, or a dragon. All reminded you of your true nature, whereby you opened yourself so far that you finally became receptive to the seed of true wisdom.

Therefore, at the moment of your enlightenment, consider whether you would like to spend some more time on Earth. For with each breath you take as an enlightened being, you bring the light of consciousness into the dream of separation, and thereby touch an infinite number of beings. Thus, every second of your embodiment can be called a service of the highest order.

Figuratively speaking, an enlightened human who is able to consciously project himself into the dream of separation becomes a mirror *that does not reflect.* Yet, he is perceived and thus becomes living proof that existence is not limited to separation! It gives an impression of existence beyond the Second Round of Creation. In other words:

The enlightened being is a window to Utopia!

In my experience, transmitting the light of true wisdom from heart to heart is the most beautiful thing to experience in the worlds of separation. It outshines even the most sublime work of art. Perhaps I was able to convey not only true wisdom, but also the feeling of beauty while transmitting it. It may motivate you to embody true wisdom, to express it in your own way, and to transmit it as well. That would be my greatest joy.

*

Last but not least, I would like to end these messages with a personal note. We – Aouwa, Althar, and Joachim – are three and we are one. Together we state:

We have fulfilled our promise!

And because it was such a joy for me, Althar, I will make another promise straight away: *I will be there whenever these messages find their way into the hands of a human.*

I am Althar, an Ambassador of Creation!

*

Acknowledgment

My heartfelt gratitude goes out to Tess "Serene" Henry for her professional and sensitive editing of the manuscript.

Thank you, Serene! It was once again great to have you on board!

Made in the USA
Monee, IL
16 September 2020